Successful
Presentation
Skills

THE SUNDAY TIMES

Successful Presentation Skills

Andrew Bradbury | Fourth Edition

LONDON   PHILADELPHIA   NEW DELHI

Publisher's note
Every possible effort has been made to ensure that the information contained in this book is accurate at the time of going to press, and the publishers and authors cannot accept responsibility for any errors or omissions, however caused. No responsibility for loss or damage occasioned to any person acting, or refraining from action, as a result of the material in this publication can be accepted by the editor, the publisher or any of the authors.

First published in 1995
Second edition 2000
Third edition 2006
Fourth edition 2010

120 Pentonville Road	525 South 4th Street, #241	4737/23 Ansari Road
London N1 9JN	Philadelphia PA 19147	Daryaganj
United Kingdom	USA	New Delhi 110002
www.koganpage.com		India

ISBN   978 0 7494 5662 7
E-ISBN   978 0 7494 5904 8

The views expressed in this book are those of the author and are not necessarily the same as those of Times Newspapers Ltd.

British Library Cataloguing-in-Publication Data

A CIP record for this book is available from the British Library.

Library of Congress Cataloging-in-Publication Data

Bradbury, Andrew (Andrew J.)
    Successful presentation skills / Andrew Bradbury. -- 4th ed.
        p. cm.
    Includes bibliographical references.
    ISBN 978-0-7494-5662-7 -- ISBN 978-0-7494-5904-8 (ebook) 1.
Business presentations. 2. Public speaking. 3. Presentation
graphics software. I. Title.
    HF5718.22.B7 2010
    658.4'52--dc22

                                                            2009042336

Typeset by Jean Cussons Typesetting, Diss, Norfolk
Printed and bound in India by Replika Press Pvt Ltd

Contents

1

Where do you want to go?

The secret of perfect presentations

Whether you're a complete novice, an experienced presenter, or somewhere in between I wonder what you want from this book?

- **Would you like to deliver a perfect presentation?**
- **Would you like your presentation to be so good that when you finish your audience gives you a standing ovation?**
- **Would you like to leave your audience with the feeling that they're 'really glad they heard that'?**

These are some of the wonderful outcomes you can (allegedly) achieve by reading other books on presentation skills. Only they may not be the 'holy grails' those books make them out to be. To explain what I mean, consider this important fact:

A study by the training department of a major computer company made a simple yet very important discovery: when the effectiveness of training courses were measured three, six and nine months after the courses ended it turned out that it was not the trainers who were rated 81 per cent and over on the 'happy sheets' who came out best. (A happy sheet is a questionnaire covering a presenter's performance, quality of the training, quality of the facilities, etc that delegates are often expected to fill in immediately after the course ends – and before they lose that warm, fluffy 'Stockholm Syndrome' feeling). On the contrary, it was the trainers who scored 61–80 per cent who really delivered the goods. It seems the top scoring trainers were being rated on their social skills rather than their ability to effectively present and transfer information.

Of course, if you never present to the same people more than once, or if you don't think anyone will ever check on the efficacy of your presentations, then getting a happy sheet score of doubtful value may not matter.

BUT

If you want to deliver quality presentations that count, presentations that people look back to months later and still think, 'Yes, that presentation really delivered the information I needed', then look no further.

What is a presentation?

Does that seem dumb? I mean, if I have to ask the question, what am I doing writing a book on the subject?

It was, of course, a 'rhetorical question,' a favourite ploy of many presenters. Instead of waiting for someone else to ask the question I want to answer, I ask the question myself, and then answer it. (See, we're only on page two and already you've learned a really useful technique!)

Of course you could just drop a question like this on your audience out of a clear blue sky like I just did. Or you could use a lead in, like, 'You may be wondering ...' or, 'If I were sitting in this audience instead of standing up here I'd probably want to ask ...', or something along those lines. And now I have asked the question, I'll go ahead and answer it.

What this means is that there is no one thing that counts as 'a presentation.' Instead we have a spectrum of events. At one end is training (concentrated on the accurate transfer of information), and speech-making (featuring pithy but possibly almost meaningless 'sound bites') is at the other, with all sorts of variations on the two themes, such as media interviews, in between. And wherever you look along the spectrum, the primary focus is on effective human-to-human communications. Which makes it rather a large subject.

In order to use the available space (in this book) as effectively as possible, the main focus will be on the sort of presentations that occur on the left-hand side of the diagram. Though quite a lot of that will also be useful, albeit in modified form, perhaps, to anyone operating in the right hand portion of the spectrum.

Ten steps to success

This book doesn't assume that the reader has any prior knowledge of the subject, and covers everything you need to know to deliver successful presentations. The layout of the book is based on a simple, 10-step process which applies to any kind of presentation:

1.   *Decide on the required outcome*. Define a clear purpose for the presentation.
2.   *Identify the audience*. Gather as much information as you can (within reason) about the people who will attend the presentation.

3. *Decide what is needed to achieve the outcome.* An effective presentation delivers as much information as the audience members actually need – not everything the presenter knows.

4. *Decide whether a presentation is the best way to meet the need(s) of the audience.* Presentations aren't the only way of communicating to groups and should only be used when they are genuinely appropriate.

5. *Collect your information.* Decide what you need to say, and collect the relevant information.

6. *Select a structure for the presentation.* Different structures are appropriate for different kinds of presentation. Decide on a suitable layout for your presentation.

7. *Prepare a script.* Create a detailed version of your presentation and decide what form it will take for you.

8. *Design and create your visual aids.* What your audience sees can be as important as what they hear. Don't settle for second best.

9. *Rehearse.* Practice really does improve performance – and has other advantages as well.

10. *Do it!* Give yourself the best chance of success in the presentation room.

Although this book covers a variety of additional information, such as confidence building, the text is primarily designed to show you how to carry through those 10 steps.

2

2, 4, 6, 8 –how do you communicate?

It's not *what* you say – is it?

One of the most expensive secrets of the business world can be summed up in two short sentences:

> Most business presentations do not achieve their intended purpose. Worse still, they frequently achieve nothing of any value!

Have you ever been in a situation where you felt that you had really presented a very convincing case for or against a certain course of action, yet nobody seemed to be the least bit affected by what you said?

This apparent failure *may* simply be due to the fact that you were saying something that nobody wanted to hear. Or you may have placed too much dependence upon the power of your words and your logic, at the expense of other aspects of your very personal contribution to the presentation.

For example, when you are trying to influence other people, how aware are you of your body language, your vocal style and your 'presence' (that vague personal quality also known as 'charm' or 'charisma')? And do you realise that your non-verbal signals may far outweigh the effect of anything you might *say*, be it in an intimate conversation or in a major presentation? Or maybe not.

The percentages – fact and fiction

One of the best-known myths in the presentation business goes like this, to quote a well-known trainer/writer:

> Professor Albert [Mehrabian]... studied social communication and discovered that communication happens on three levels:
>
> - Visual – 55% (body language)
> - Vocal – 38% (tone of voice)
> - Verbal – 7% (words)

By far, visual communication is the most powerful of the three types.

Similar information regularly appears in any number of locations in books and online, even though it isn't true. The figures are correct – it's the explanation of the figures that is in error.

What Mehrabian reported was much more specific than the above quote suggests. In practice, the figures *only* apply when the speaker is *'communicating feelings or attitudes to others'*. Moreover, the findings only apply to situations when we have to 'resolv[e] the general meaning or impact of an *inconsistent message'* (Albert Mehrabian, *Silent Messages* 2nd edn, 1981, Wadsworth, Belmont, CA. Italics added for emphasis).

It's the way that you say it

This does not mean that we can ignore body language and tone of voice, however. Anyone who thinks that once they've got their body language right the words don't really matter runs the risk of producing a very poor presentation.

Moreover, we may not fully understand what our non-verbal signals mean to other people.

For example, how well do you know your own voice? Is it deep and gruff, about average or a little high pitched? Do you speak quickly, slowly or at a medium pace? Do you have an extensive range of tones and inflections which make your voice interesting to listen to or (be honest) does your voice tend to become rather monotonous if you have to speak continuously for more than four or five minutes?

In the United Kingdom and the United States, a person who speaks slowly and in a lower-than-average tone is widely perceived as being powerful and credible. Someone with a faster, higher-toned voice will be seen as enthusiastic but lightweight through to positively untrustworthy.

By the same token, a person whose gestures are few and far between is seen as being powerful, deliberate and intelligent. The sort of person who makes frequent, expansive gestures may be seen as frivolous or even a couple of sandwiches short of a picnic.

I'm really pleased to be here – maybe

Here's a simple example of how Mehrabian's findings might work in practice. Imagine that you have been invited to attend the launch of a new product which the manufacturers hope will be a world-beater. After a rather long wait, a door opens and a man enters and walks wearily to the podium set up at the front of the room. He is tall, and well dressed in dark suit, white shirt and discreetly patterned tie. His hair is carefully styled and his shoes look smart, well polished and expensive. He reaches the podium, and waits for a minute or so with shoulders bowed, grasping the sides of the lectern as though his life depended on it. He stares down at his notes and *avoids* establishing eye contact with the audience as he makes his opening remarks in a voice that is tired and monotonous, even depressed:

> Good morning, ladies and gentlemen. May I start by saying how nice it is to see such a large audience. I think I can safely promise you a very interesting and stimulating day...

Do *you* believe that he is pleased to see you? Do *you* believe his promise that the events which are to follow will be interesting and stimulating? Are you looking forward to what is to come – or working out how to make an inconspicuous but speedy exit?

I suspect that your answers would indicate some very low expectations. Yet this cannot be due to what was *said*. Taking the words out of context, the message they convey is polite, positive and even enthusiastic. But if the verbal content is combined with the incongruent vocal signals and body language, it is the signals and body language that we believe, not the verbal content.

Of course this works the other way round as well. Congruence between the messages from the three channels may be unconsciously taken as evidence that the speaker is being truthful when maybe they aren't.

Some years ago, researchers from USC and Southern Illinois University medical schools ran three seminars on *Mathematical Game Theory as Applied to Physical Education*. A total of 55 people attended the three talks, including psychologists, psychiatrists, educators and social workers. What no one realised was that the presenter, a 'Dr Myron L Fox' was not the 'outstanding psychiatrist' many of them judged him to be – he was a carefully schooled actor with absolutely no medical qualifications. And not one member of the three audiences spotted that the talk itself was a cleverly scripted combination of a 'pop science' article and a liberal helping of doubletalk, non sequiturs, and contradictory and irrelevant statements, plus a generous helping of humour. In other words – almost pure nonsense.

In short, the most brilliant speech ever written will ultimately depend for its success on the *presentation style* of the *speech-maker* and not just on the *contents* of the speech itself.

No matter what the situation, if your *style* of presentation isn't an audience-grabber the *content* begins to become irrelevant. Indeed, a truly unskilled presenter can put their material across in such a way that the members of the audience not only don't take it in, they don't even *care* that they haven't taken it in. They are just glad when the presentation is over.

A powerful real life example of this phenomenon at work must be the pre-election debate between John F Kennedy and Richard M Nixon when the two men were competing for the post of President of the United States back in 1960.

Those people who only *heard* the debate on radio had to rely on the verbal content and vocal signals to guide their perceptions. Most *listeners* regarded Nixon as the better candidate.

Of the people who *saw* the debate on television, and thus received verbal content and the vocal signals and saw the body language of the two speakers, the majority perceived John F Kennedy as being a far more credible candidate.

It is a simple fact of history that it was Nixon who had the policies, but Kennedy who won the presidency!

The presenter who can create rapport with their audience is operating on both the conscious *and* the subconscious levels. At its best the effect can be quite magical. The good news is that there is nothing 'magical' about it. It is a skill which almost anyone can master with a little time and effort.

3

When you feel the fear...

Panic now – and avoid the rush

You're sitting quietly at your desk when suddenly the call comes: 'We need a presentation, and only *you* can do it!' What do you feel? Pride? Caution? Or unadulterated

PANIC

Since most people are likely to opt for *panic*, why not turn this to your advantage by using it as a five-part reminder of the key elements of a good presentation:

Outline your	**P**urpose
Analyse your	**A**udience
Identify the	**N**eed
Collate your	**I**nformation
Prepare your	**C**ommunication

Purpose

In many cases the purpose of a presentation will not be a matter of choice – it will be dictated for you by someone else or by the context in which the presentation will take place:

- Your department head asks you to show Sally Gorringe (a new employee) the ropes.
- You are chosen to give senior management a brief overview of the work done by your team.
- It is your task to round out the proceedings at a sales conference in a positive and motivating fashion.

On Monday morning Bob's boss, Mark, called him in and told him that he was going to be doing a presentation on their latest product ('Product X') for the benefit of some customers who would be visiting the company's offices on Thursday afternoon.

On Thursday afternoon Bob waited patiently in the meeting room that had been set aside for his presentation. Eventually, at 4.45 pm, Bob's boss and the eight visitors trooped into the room. With little more than a nod to Bob, Mark showed the visitors to their seats, took his place at the front of the room, said a few words to introduce Bob – and sat down.

Bob, making the best he could of the situation, ran through some historical information about why the company had decided to bring this particular product to market. He brought in some background material on the development of Product X, and he rounded things off by announcing the intended preview and release dates for Product X.

The next day, Mark called Bob into his office again, but not to congratulate him.

'What the blue blazes was all that about?' Mark demanded. 'I spent the whole afternoon taking those guys round the factory, showing them how Product X was developed and so on. And when we get to your presentation they have to sit through a cut-down version of the same material!

'All I wanted from you was a nice little piece, about 10 to 15 minutes long, to round out everything I'd been saying and to encourage them to place some hefty advance orders!'

In order to produce a successful presentation you must have a clear idea of what the presentation is to be about. Furthermore, your understanding must be both precise and accurate. If necessary, push for further information until you are sure that you fully and accurately understand that purpose:

- **Are you required to train Sally Gorringe in some specific tasks, or simply to familiarise her with the general routine?**
- **Are you doing a solo presentation to senior management, or are you one of half a dozen speakers?**
- **What are the current sales figures like? Will your own presentation be preceded by rewards or recriminations?**

Many a good presentation has fallen by the wayside because the speaker wasn't sufficiently clear about his purpose.

Audience

In each of those examples a specific audience has been mentioned each time – the new employee, senior management and the sales team. And one of the first things you should do when preparing for any presentation is find out as much as you can about your intended audience, and then focus your presentation accordingly.

Even if you aren't able to meet any of the members of your audience in advance, you can still use a simple but surprisingly powerful test to make a pretty accurate estimate of what they will be like using these questions:

Q1:   If I'm describing a new idea to you, would you prefer that I start with (a) the details, or (b) the big picture?

Q2a: If you answered (a) to question 1, would you like me to (c) work up from the details to the bigger picture, or (d) stick with the details?

Q2b: If you answered (b) to question 1, would you want me to (e) work down to a more detailed description, or (f) stick with the big picture?

Someone who answered (a) and (d) obviously prefers to work with details, whereas a person who selected (b) and (f) is likely to be much more comfortable dealing in generalities. A person who selects (a) and (c) is primarily detail-oriented, but is also interested to see how those details relate to the big picture. Finally, someone who selects (b) and (e) will probably prefer to work in generalities, whilst being able to deal with more precise details when this is appropriate.

We can apply these conclusions to job roles to estimate what kind of presentation style the corresponding job-holders might prefer.

Most senior managers and board members are required to think in terms of long-term company strategy for the next five years, and competition at the national and international level. Such people are therefore likely to select answers (b) and limited (e) – indicating a fairly non-detailed type of presentation. Staff in the R&D department, on the other hand, are more likely to answer (a) and (d), which would call for lots of facts and figures in either the presentation or in the supporting handout.

A presentation at a Sales Conference might tend to be (b) and (f) if the main purpose is to celebrate the year's results, or (b) and very limited (e) at the rollout of a new product.

If you're still not sure what approach to adopt, you might try starting with a reasonably high level overview, then work down to a medium degree of detail. And leave plenty of time for people to ask questions.

Need

Every presentation has a *purpose*, and answers a *need or needs*. The *purpose* of taking Sally Gorringe through the office procedures may be to bring her up to speed in her job as quickly as possible, but what are her *needs*? Does she need detailed instructions, or just a brief refresher?

And what do *you* need in order to be able to meet this requirement? Can you 'do it with your eyes shut'? Or do you need to do some research? Is this a routine situation, or a chance to put yourself in line for promotion?

The more clearly you can define the *needs* of the situation, the more chance you have of giving a really 'spot on' presentation.

Information

So, you now know who your presentation is for, and why. But what information should be included to achieve the required outcome? If you give too little information the event becomes a waste of everyone's time. Give too much information and most of it will be forgotten by the next day – and the event becomes a waste of everyone's time.

The more accurately you define your goal, the easier it will be to determine what must go into the presentation – and what can be left out. And if, indeed, a presentation is actually necessary.

Communication

What visual aids will you use (if any)? Where will the presentation be staged? What kind of follow-up will be required?

This is where you plan the *framework* for your presentation, and consider the crucial question: How will it be perceived by your audience (will they hear what you *meant* to say, what you *did* say, what they *think* you said or what they *think* you meant by what they *think* they heard you say)?

Your 'performing edge'

It is quite normal to feel some degree of apprehension when you are about to embark on an activity that is both important and, to a certain extent, unknown. Will the audience be responsive? Will your presentation be appropriate to their needs? Will the mains power supply flow smoothly?

As Kipling might have put it, if he's been in a more humorous mood:

> If you can keep your head when all about are losing theirs –
> You probably don't know what's going on!

A presenter who doesn't feel any apprehension before an event is generally, in my experience, not nearly as skilled in delivering presentations as they think they are.

The 'secret' remedy for so-called stage fright is to acknowledge the feeling without letting it upset you. Trying to ignore those feelings is self-defeating, because you have to keep thinking about the feelings in order to remember what it is you are trying to ignore!

So if you do feel a little nervous, 'reframe' that feeling. Reinterpret what is happening to you as a process of revving up for a really successful performance. Remind yourself that a little extra adrenalin is not only normal – it helps to give you a 'performing edge'. Then concentrate on all the things that you are going to do to make this your best presentation yet.

Winning ways

A genuinely effective way to acquire new skills is to find out what acknowledged experts do, understand what makes them successful, and then apply that behaviour in your own life – and thereby learn to duplicate that success.

A county council in Southern England planned to install a new computer system across all of their libraries, but who would do the training? As is often the case, the budget wouldn't stretch to bringing in outside trainers to do everything; and in any case, outsiders wouldn't have a very clear idea of what kind of changes the introduction of a new system would involve.

So it was decided to train up existing librarians to do the 'end user training'. This meant that a single expert trainer could be brought in to give more in-depth attention over a longer period of time, to the 12 trainers-to-be.

The result was highly satisfactory all round with the 'trainer to trainer' course being more thorough than any standard offering and the librarians-turned-trainers being genuinely fully prepared right from the start of the end user training sessions.

The following list sets out the five skills most frequently used by people rated by their colleagues as outstanding presenters:

Fine-tuning
Outcome-oriented
Chunking
Unlimited points of view
Success assurance

- **Fine-tuning**
  A skilled presenter constantly hones and refines their material to make it as appropriate as possible for a given audience. This process continues until the very end of the event, and the presenter will repeatedly check that the presentation is headed in the right direction, using their skill and *flexibility* to adapt the style, tempo and focus of the presentation in order to achieve their original objectives.
- **Achieving outcomes**
  If you don't know where you want to go, how will you know which route to take? And how will you know when you've arrived? Top presenters work to answer two basic questions right from the start of the planning stage:
  - What do I want the presentation to achieve?
  - How will the audience behave if I am achieving my outcome?
- **Effective chunking**
  'Chunking' is an essential skill which might be described as 'the process of presenting information in manageable segments'. Some people like to start with an overview and work down to the nitty-gritty, and others will prefer to start with the details and build up to the big picture.

  Skilled presenters most frequently *chunk* downwards. That is to say, they start with an overview and work down to the details. They also watch for audience reactions which will tell them if they are working in the right direction and at the right pace.

- Unlimited points of view
  Many top speakers give their presentations from *three* different positions: Position 1 is their own viewpoint, Position 2 is the audience's viewpoint, and Position 3 is the 'neutral observer' or 'fly on the wall' position.

  By mentally switching from one position to another they can give their presentation a personal dimension (Position 1), they can judge how they are coming across to the audience (Position 2), and they can avoid any conflict or confrontation, should it arise, by moving to Position 3. This particular skill takes time to develop, but it is an amazingly effective key to handling any kind of audience and any kind of situation.
- What *must* be, *will* be
  The fifth characteristic common to most skilful presenters is an unshakeable belief that each presentation is bound to be successful, no matter what happens. It is as though they are saying to themselves, albeit quite unconsciously: 'This is the outcome I *require* – therefore it *will* occur.'

It must be seen to be believed

Before you read on, recall an incident from your past which is associated with very strong *positive* emotions – winning a prize, the first time you fell in love or whatever. Remember as much as you can about the event. Bring to mind the sights, sounds, physical feelings and so on. Then come back to the present and take stock of your state of mind.

How do you feel now? Possibly a lot better than when you started to read this section. Yet nothing actually happened. Your emotional reactions were triggered by a memory, not by an actual event.

You have just demonstrated a very simple form of the technique known as *visualisation*, and its power to generate positive emotions.

Visualisation can also be used to focus your efforts more effectively by creating a mental image of a desired event *as though it had already happened!* There is nothing magical about the process, it is based on a simple psychological fact:

> Our brains store all memories in the same manner and therefore – as demonstrated by researchers such as Professor Elizabeth Loftus – cannot tell from the memory alone the difference between a past experience and a fictional event, be it read, heard, seen or imagined.

Effective visualisation is simply a way of convincing our brain that something imagined is, in fact, real. The more vividly we imagine the event, the more the brain is convinced that the event must be real – and integrates it with our existing memories as though it was a *remembered fact!*

The pudding of proof

Please understand that visualisation is unlikely to work if you try to convince yourself about something you don't really believe is possible. For the best results, set yourself realistic goals and build upon them as your belief grows.

Concentrate on your own actions and feelings. As a daily activity, build up an increasingly detailed mental image of yourself delivering the presentation in an effective manner.

Tell yourself that you are going to do the best job you can on this presentation, that you are going to be successful, and that you *deserve* that success. You will be amazed at the strength of belief in yourself which develops when you regularly practise this technique.

By the way, you will find that your visualisation is even more effective if you can spend some time in the room where the presentation will take place. If it is at all possible, do take the opportunity to get the 'feel' of the room – its size, the level of any background noise, the seating layout and so on. Stroll around the room as though you owned the place. Do whatever it takes to make your visualisation as realistic as it can be.

Focus your attention on generating positive images and feelings about your role in the presentation. If the whole visualisation process seems a bit strange at first, go with it, this is perfectly normal and won't prevent you from achieving a beneficial result. After only a few days you will begin to notice changes in your attitude to the presentation, and before long you'll actually be looking forward to it.

Pictures and images

Before reading this next section, please close your eyes and imagine relaxing on a beautiful sandy beach. Take particular note of the first thing that comes to mind.

Now, what was that first thought? Was it a picture, of silver sand, gentle waves on the sea, a clear blue sky or whatever? Was it a sound, of waves splashing gently on the shore, perhaps? Or was it a feeling, of fine sand beneath your feet or the warmth of the sun on your body, for example?

If the first thought was some kind of picture then your foremost representational mode at that moment was *visual*. If your first thought was of something you could hear then your foremost representational mode was *auditory*. And if your first thought was about how you felt (either physically or emotionally), then your foremost representational mode was *kinaesthetic*.

> **Note:** Our *representational systems* are basically our five senses: sight, sound, feelings/touch, smell and taste. Our foremost representational system is the channel we take most notice of when collecting and processing information about the world around us. Our foremost representational system may well vary from context to content. Thus it is appropriate to talk of someone as being in visual/auditory/ kinaesthetic mode rather than 'visual people' or 'auditory people', etc.
>
> Some people may find that they use two representational systems more or less simultaneously. This is often the case, and for the purposes of the discussion which follows, those representational systems should be regarded as equal in importance.

In the last couple of sections I've deliberately referred to mental *images* rather than mental pictures. People often think that 'visualisation' has to be based on literally seeing pictures in your mind. This is not, in fact, correct.

For reasons explained elsewhere in this book (see beginning of chapter 10, for example), visual images are indeed a powerful way of conveying ideas. But some of us seldom use 'visual' as our foremost representational system, and calling up mental pictures is easier for some people than for others.

In practice your visualisation should be based on whichever representational system seems most comfortable in the context. A visualisation based primarily on sound or feelings will work just as well as one based on pictures. What matters is simply that you use the representational system that 'comes naturally' rather than trying to force yourself to think in a way that creates resistance.

4

Confidence matters

You're never alone in a presentation – it just feels like that

Are you a good letter writer? Do you feel comfortable dealing with people over the phone?

If you answered 'yes' to either of these questions you have already learned to deal with the presenter's Number One nightmare: *lack of feedback*.

In a face-to-face conversation we are provided with a stream of almost instantaneous signals, both verbal and non-verbal, which let us know how the other person or people in the conversation are reacting to what we are saying.

During a telephone conversation the *physical* non-verbal signals are entirely absent, and we must take our cues from the other person's tone of voice and choice of words. Given that many people have a quite distinct 'telephone manner', even these verbal signals aren't always entirely reliable, however, and this is one reason why some people prefer not to deal with important and sensitive matters over the phone.

When it comes to writing a letter we get no feedback whatever, of course, which is why so many adults tend to write letters that are nearly as clipped and brief as a telegram.

Fortunately, in terms of the feedback received, a presentation ranks higher than both making a phone call and writing a letter. And that's important, because surveys have shown that many people tend to treat no feedback as *negative feedback!*

Yet there is absolutely no reason why this should be the case.

> **Martin gave a presentation to a group of 30–40 people at his company's head office. He started badly, fussing with his OHP foils and vainly trying to get the projected image 'squared up' on the screen. He was clearly ill at ease, and his opening remarks were liberally peppered with 'ers', 'ums' and 'ahs'.**
>
> **Then, after the first few minutes, the presentation suddenly began to improve quite noticeably in pace and clarity. Martin had somehow overcome his initial nervousness and was now in full control of the event.**
>
> **The only other aspect of Martin's behaviour that noticeably changed was the way that he seemed to look at one particular section of the audience more often than any other. But even that wasn't very noticeable unless you were looking for it.**

Across a crowded room

So what miracle saved Martin's presentation from disaster?

No miracle. Martin simply found a friendly face, someone who leaned forward in their seat, who seemed to be hanging on every word he said, and who laughed at his witticisms.

The poor start was primarily due to Martin's feelings of isolation, of being 'on the spot'. He allowed his negative feelings to take the upper hand and showed his lack of confidence. The audience picked up on these non-verbal messages and their body language reflected their own negative feelings. It was very fortunate that Martin kept his wits about him so that, when he did find a friendly face, he was able to establish a positive rapport with that member of the audience. From that point on, he was able to pull himself back from the brink of disaster and deliver a satisfactory presentation.

The aura effect

This is not to say that Martin spent the rest of the presentation talking to just that one person, of course.

The most basic link between any two people is *eye contact*. It is important, then, that you maintain more or less continuous eye contact with the whole of your audience. Two key elements which ensure dynamic eye contact with an audience are *timing* and the *Aura Effect*.

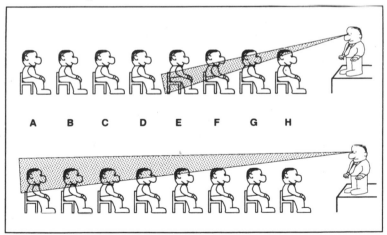

The Aura Effect works because our field of vision appears to 'fan out' as it gets farther away, extending to the sides, in front of and behind the person the presenter is actually looking at. Thus, in the upper part of the illustration, when the presenter makes eye contact with one person near the front of the audience (in row

G), about nine people (three people in rows F, G and H) are likely to think that he is looking at them. When the presenter looks towards the back of the audience, however, as many as 15 to 20 people are likely to believe that the presenter is looking at them and them alone.

It isn't necessary, then, to look at every single member of the audience in order to maintain effective contact. Indeed, the Aura Effect allows you to maintain rapport with whole groups of people rather than with isolated individuals. Moreover, it is seldom the case that a presenter will find only one friendly face in an audience of any size. In practice a fair number of the people in your audience will be taking an active interest in what you are saying, and that they will be reasonably spread out rather than all sitting together in a single block.

So we aren't really cut off from any kind of feedback when we give a presentation after all – it just feels like that. The real problem is that we get relatively little feedback, and what we do get is often of a type that we seldom if ever consciously recognise, namely '*non*-verbal signals'.

That certain look

Imagine that you are giving a presentation right this minute. You look out at your audience and you notice a woman in her mid- to late thirties, sitting slightly to your right, who has her left leg crossed comfortably over the right so that the left knee is pointing more or less in your direction. Her head is tilted slightly to her right and upwards. Her right hand is resting against her cheek, with the fingers loosely closed, except the index finger, which is pointing straight upwards.

Now, if I say that the woman is looking bright and interested, it won't take much thought to realise that the woman's attitude is positive. But we can actually interpret the meaning of this *cluster* of body signals much more precisely than that.

The woman's overall deportment is signalling interest and

approval. Crossed legs, with the upper knee towards someone, generally indicates interest in that person (the crossed leg position is only negative when the legs are firmly 'locked'). The hand-to-face gesture is also a sign of positive evaluation, as long as the head is not being supported and the mouth is not covered. The head slightly tilted to one side is another indication of interest, as compared to the downward tilted head, which is associated with a negative or critical attitude. The cluster as a whole (and body language must be taken 'as a whole' to have any chance of arriving at an accurate interpretation) says that this member of the audience is on your side, you 'share the same language'.

When you look out at your audience, far from giving you no feedback, they are actually sending you a whole host of messages if only you can recognise them.

Nor do you need to be an expert in reading body language in order to use it as a confidence booster. The only gestures that are worth spotting, in this context, are the positive ones. Like Martin you should look out for the friendly, approving, interested members of your audience, then work to increase the rapport between those people and yourself. As the enthusiasm builds, because of the Aura Effect other members of the audience will find it hard not to become involved.

Body language is not an infallible guide to human behaviour, of course. The person whom you might think looks bored stiff could just have had a late night. And the person who spends their time apparently doodling and who never looks up during the entire presentation may just be taking notes in the form of Mind Maps.

Make it a habit to always look for the most positive interpretation of any audience behaviour, however odd, or even bizarre, it may be at times. It is important that you learn how to generate confidence from within, rather than depending upon the audience to help you out. And for that you need to *be* confident.

Ready, willing and able

It is a good idea to start working on any presentation as soon as you have a clear idea of what is required. Even if you are rerunning a previously delivered presentation, check through your materials.

Are your visual aids as clear and interesting as they could be? Have any of the 'facts' in the presentation changed since you last delivered it? Is there anything you can add, remove or alter to make the presentation more interesting, more useful or more appropriate to the next audience?

To have prepared your presentation as fully as possible, with a tightly edited script, sufficient visual aids and plenty of rehearsal time, is a tremendous confidence builder. It will give you a sense of being in control of your material that you can never get from trying to do everything at the last moment.

A sense of perspective

A second key confidence builder is having a realistic appreciation of your *current* strengths.

Decide what kind of presentation you are capable of delivering. Are you happy about working with a flipchart, or do you prefer to use previously prepared foils on an overhead or computer-linked projector? Do you need to work from some kind of cue cards or script, or are you comfortable speaking without notes? If possible have a chat with someone else in the company whom you regard as being a capable or even talented presenter, and don't be too polite to pick their brains.

And finally, when you think you know your own capabilities, aim just a bit higher. According to a detailed study carried out some years ago, the average person is successful in approximately 95 per cent of the tasks they undertake. The biggest single cause of failure is not having tried in the first place!

The look, the feel, the sound

As we saw in chapter 00, we all process our views of the world through a series of filters – auditory, visual and kinaesthetic. Thus when we are having something explained to us we might say 'That *sounds* OK to me', or 'Now I *see* what mean' or 'That *strikes* me as a good idea'. We unconsciously select words that express the way we're thinking (our representational system) and we respond most positively to people who seem to be using the same filter(s) that we are using, a case of 'seeing eye to eye', 'being in tune' or 'having certain feelings in common'.

A presenter who only uses the phraseology of their own representational system may be creating rapport with as few as one-third of the members of their audience. The other two-thirds, though they may never know why, are likely to feel 'out of tune' with the presenter, won't share their 'point of view', or may simply not be able to 'grasp' the meaning of what is being said.

Hand signals should be observed

People frequently make small but easily discernible movements that effectively 'point out' their preferred thinking style at that particular moment in time. For example:

- **Rubbing or pointing to the area around the eyes indicates a *visual* representational system. That person probably 'doesn't *see* what you're getting at'. Or perhaps they have '*spotted*' something in one of your OHP foils that '*looks* rather interesting'.**
- **Any noticeable movement around the ears or the mouth indicates an *auditory* representational system at work. If someone starts pulling at their earlobe, this may indicate that they don't 'like what they *hear*', but on the other hand, they may be thinking that 'there's a lot in what you *say*'.**

- Gestures with the arms and/or hands (such as rubbing an arm or a leg, or unnecessary adjustments to items of clothing) usually accompany a *kinaesthetic* response. That person may 'feel that the point you have just made needs *fleshing out*', or they may think that your ideas have given them 'something to get to *grips* with'.

As to whether a particular gesture should be interpreted as a sign of approval or dissent, the expression on the person's face should make that clear for you.

Turning theory into practice

Understanding your audience is yet another source of confidence – knowing both *who* will be attending the presentation, and, just as importantly, *why*?

Some time ago I went on a tour of the United Kingdom with two of my colleagues, giving presentations on a new piece of software our company had produced. Over a period of three months we did the same presentations nearly two dozen times, from Bristol to Edinburgh, from Cardiff to London. And we didn't meet a single delegate before the moment when they first came through the door of the presentation room. So how on earth did we ever manage to *analyse our audience*?

The first thing we decided was that delegates would probably be very mixed in the ways that they would process the information we were giving them. That is to say, we took it as read that our presentations had to consist of a mixture of auditory, visual and kinaesthetic material. In order to adequately inform our audiences about the new software we had to *tell* them what it did, we had to *show* them what it looked like. Then we had to give them some '*hands on*' practical experience so that they *felt comfortable* with it and would take a positive message back to their companies.

We also used the three styles in the very words we used to

present our information, so that they could '*hear* what was on offer', '*see* what we meant', and '*grasp* the basic concepts that *underpinned* the design of the new software'.

Focused motivation

Another important consideration was how to motivate delegates to buy in to using this new software – which constituted a major change from their previously paper-based procedures.

Contrary to what some books might have you believe, there is no one way to motivate an entire audience. On the contrary, it is much more realistic to think of motivation in terms of a sliding scale between two basic viewpoints, such as *towards* and *away from*, for example.

In very basic terms, when someone is in *towards* mode they are motivated by what they can *achieve*. When a person is in *away* from mode they are mainly concerned with the things they want to avoid. (The average split in a typical business audience is about 40 per cent *towards*, 40 per cent *away from*, and 20 per cent somewhere in between.)

In this particular case, we knew that many companies were adopting the new software because they feared losing out if they didn't accept the new practices – a mainly *away from* attitude. We weren't dealing with the companies, however, but with individual end users – whose personal views might be quite different from those of their company.

On this basis we covered both sides of the story; the potential dangers of not taking on the new software, and also the many potential benefits that computerisation would bring.

The question behind the question

Making this distinction was especially useful when it came to the question and answer sessions. Instead of adopting a sort of middle-of-the-road approach to every question, we answered each questioner in their own style, and added a little rider at the end of each answer to cater for people with another style.

So, one question that came up several times, in one form or another, went something like this:

> Isn't this going to involve a whole extra learning curve for the people who have to use the software?

Phrased in this way, the question contains the implication that there is something (extra learning) that the questioner would rather not have to deal with (ie *away from* thinking). To meet the questioner on their own ground our answer was therefore mainly *away from*, with an element of *towards*:

> Yes, there certainly will be a learning curve, though it is unlikely to be anything like as steep as some people might imagine. [Since the 'someone' is not specifically identified, this sentence will assure everyone in the audience that the learning curve won't be as steep as they expect].
>
> The alternative option [away from people don't usually like having options, so this is a double whammy for them] is to carry on with your current methods and get left behind by the companies who do adopt this new way of working. And we all know what getting left behind can mean these days – a fall off in business, downsizing and so on.
>
> Of course the good news is that companies who accept the need for an extra investment in time and training can expect to see substantial returns on that investment!

Note: Handling audience questions is dealt with in detail in Chapter 13.

How to create confidence

As well as building confidence through being well prepared and through understanding your audience, there are also ways of directly installing and boosting your own confidence.

Relaxation

Firstly, a simple relaxation technique. For best results take a relaxation break every day:

1. Find somewhere quiet where you can be free of disturbances for 10–20 minutes (10 minutes is OK, 20 minutes is more than twice as effective).
2. All you need is a comfortable seat, preferably with arm rests, but not so comfortable that you will be tempted to fall asleep.
3. At a convenient time (more or less the same time each day is preferable, but not essential) go to this quiet place and sit in the chair with your arms on the arm rests, feet firmly on the floor and legs slightly apart.
4. Close your eyes and take a minute or two to get used to any of the little noises that may occur.
5. When you are ready, start to pay attention to your breathing by counting from 1 to 10 – breathe in (1), breathe out (2), breathe in (3) and so on. When you get to 10, start again from 1.
6. If your attention wanders at any time simply start counting again from 1 on your next in breath.

Not only is this process beneficial to your overall health, it has the added advantage that, after a few sessions, doing it for just two or three minutes shortly before a presentation is enough to put you in a calm and resourceful state.

The circle of excellence

The second technique is generally known as 'the circle of excellence', and is incredibly effective. You can do it on your own if you wish, though many people find it easier if they have someone read the instructions to them:

1. Find a quiet place where you will not be overlooked or disturbed for about 5–10 minutes.
2. Decide exactly what 'state' you want to install – calmness, competence, feeling motivated and so on.
3. Stand somewhere in the middle of this space in a comfortable pose and gently shake both arms, then each leg in turn, just to loosen up and 'break state', as it's sometimes called.
4. Imagine that there is a circle on the floor in front of you about 1 metre (3 feet) across. If you cannot 'see' the circle just be comfortable with the idea that it is there.
5. Then imagine that it is filled with your favourite colour.
6. With your eyes open or shut, whichever you prefer, imagine a relevant situation and what it would be like if you were in exactly the state you want to be in. Think of how you would like to feel and what you might be seeing and hearing. If you can actually recall a previous experience of being in the desired state – in this case being competent – so much the better. Remember the point made in Chapter 3 – the more vividly we imagine an event, the more readily the brain will 'remember' it as though it actually happened.
7. Think of an appropriate word or a short phrase such as 'Now' or 'I'm ready.'
8. When the memory seems to be reaching full strength, step forward into the circle, whilst repeating your 'trigger' – under your breath is a good idea if you are likely to use it when other people are around.
9. As the feeling begins to fade, if you have your eyes closed, open them. Remember the experience for a moment or two, then step out of the circle and do the short 'break state' exercise (see Step 3).
10. Rerun the process several times. You will normally find that by the second or third repeat you can simply step into the circle and the feeling of confidence will kick in more or less automatically with little or no conscious effort on your part.

When it comes to the actual event imagine the coloured circle in front of you and then step into it, whilst saying the 'trigger'. Then deliver a truly effective presentation.

5

The main objective

Is this really necessary?

Many business presentations take several days to prepare, especially when very sophisticated graphics are involved. And many more hours are involved in delivering the presentations (taking account of the delegates' time as well as that of the presentation team). And in more cases than anyone is likely to admit, the core information could have been presented far more effectively as a memo or a small document of six pages or less.

So, once you know the purpose of your preparation, a vital first step is to ask yourself: 'Is a presentation the *best* way of achieving the required objective?' Check it against the following indicators:

- **Do people need to be able to discuss the topic of the presentation in order to reach a decision?**
- **Do people need to be able to question the presenter in order to fully understand the material?**

- Is the presentation necessary to 'sell' an idea, a product or a course of action?
- Is there any kind of practical element in the presentation?

If there is no obvious need to deliver information in person then staging a presentation may only be a second best solution.

Roy was asked to prepare a presentation for some of the senior managers. Unfortunately, he was already under pressure to wrap up an existing assignment, and the time needed to prepare and deliver the presentation could seriously jeopardise the chances of meeting the deadline for the current project. Roy decided to review the situation and examine the real goal that he was being asked to achieve, which was simply to disseminate information.

Instead of preparing a script, Roy drew up a wholly adequate *written* description of the required information including half a dozen relevant charts and diagrams. The whole package was put together in a couple of evenings, typed up during the day – whilst Roy was getting on with his other work – and was delivered to head office a couple of days earlier than the proposed presentation.

He didn't need time to turn hard facts into a speech, or to rehearse, or prepare visual aids. He didn't have to be out of the office for a whole day when time was scarce. The senior managers also benefited by being able to review the material at their leisure and didn't have to put off any last minute appointments that would have clashed with the presentation.

So never *assume* that a presentation is the only way or the best way to communicate information until you've considered all the other options.

And the point is?

If you do decide that a presentation is necessary, there are at least five or six possible formats, again depending on your purpose. To decide which is most appropriate it will be a big help if you start by describing your primary objective *in just one sentence*. Something like:

- **inform all the members of the project as to the current state of play;**
- **convince senior management that the flexitime system should be extended to include *all* office staff;**
- **explain why the current production targets are unattainable, and to present a more realistic set of figures;**
- **motivate the sales force to get behind the company's new product lines.**

Give this definition of your primary objective some hard thought, and don't go on until you are satisfied that it is as precise and accurate as you can make it. Then stick to it.

Once you know what you aim to say, you are ready to determine what the presentation is meant to achieve. For example:

- **to gather people's views – on a new product, on moves to reshape the company, or whatever;**
- **to make people aware of an idea or to describe a business opportunity – to gain support for some course of action, or to indicate that action will be required in the future;**

- to sell something or to persuade people to take a course of action which they might not wish to take;
- to highlight a problem – to seek a solution, or at least to minimise its effect;
- to pass on information – to report progress or promote awareness (without requiring any kind of response);
- in education or training – to enhance productivity, encourage a more productive/flexible/efficient work ethic.

Now we need to set out the expected/required *result* of the presentation as clearly as possible.

Lend me your brains

No matter *why* we want to gather people's opinions on any topic, there are certain basic targets that must be set:

- **Everyone involved must clearly understand the nature of the presentation.**
- **Everyone must understand what input is expected from them.**
- **In this kind of presentation you will probably want to have a medium to high degree of audience interaction – to have people build on each other's ideas – but without splitting off into a series of unofficial discussions.**
- **The presenter(s) must have some kind of yardstick so that they can tell when the presentation has achieved its goals (or at least has gone as far as it can usefully go).**

The basic framework for such a presentation might look something like this:

- **Introduce the presentation – motivate the audience.**
- **Describe what is to be discussed, why, and the required objective(s).**

- Open the topic up to discussion.
- Summarise the outcome of the discussion or, for a pre-defined period of time, divide the audience into a number of 'official' discussion groups.
- If appropriate, give some indication of the likely outcome of the presentation.

I have a dream

When presenting a new idea, your main objectives may be:

- to have the members of the audience clearly understand the new idea;
- to gain acceptance for the new idea;
- to obtain a commitment to implement the new idea.

In order to achieve these goals the basic outline of your presentation might look something like this:

- Introduce the presentation giving some idea of its purpose – including the need for decision and commitment.
- Describe the *need* for the new idea – does it represent sequential progress or diversification?
- Describe the idea.
- Describe the results and benefits which might reasonably follow the adoption of the new idea.
- Summarise your main points and give clear guidelines on what people should do to support the new idea.

Roll up, roll up!

In a sense *all* presentations are a form of selling – selling information, ideas, solutions and so on. In a deliberately *persuasive* presentation you will need to include some or all of the following elements:

- **The members of the audience must understand what is being asked of them.**
- **They must accept the need for the proposed action.**
- **Regardless of whether the audience accepts every word of the arguments you are putting forward, they must be persuaded to *act* in the required manner.**

This is potentially the most difficult kind of presentation and must be handled with tact. Nevertheless, a carefully (and correctly) structured presentation can anticipate any negative reactions and actively encourage your audience to 'buy in' to the proposed action rather than fighting against it:

- **Introduction. Briefly identify the subject of the presentation, with strong emphasis on any common interests that may be involved – to keep the business running, to reduce costs, and so on.**
- **Explain why *any* action needs to be taken. Be as frank and as open as possible. And if certain information needs to be withheld to protect the company's commercial interests, then say so. Don't pretend you are being totally open if you aren't.**
- **Explain exactly what action needs to be taken, and by whom, showing (if possible) how you have reduced any negative element(s) to a minimum.**
- **Emphasise the *positive* elements of the course of action.**
- **Summarise the contents of your presentation and call for agreement on the proposals.**

No problem too great

When the key element of a presentation relates to a problem, we might approach it in one of three ways, depending on what we have to say about the problem, and what action (if any) we want from other people:

- Highlight the problem as a matter of information;
- Open the topic up for discussion and possible solutions; or
- Offer a solution to the problem, for further discussion.

In each case our primary aim must be to foster understanding of the problem, and in two and three we would also want to:

- discuss the pros and cons of the possible solutions;
- gain agreement on what should be done about the problem/solution(s).

The presentation might contain the following elements:

- Introduction. Make it clear whether the presentation is intended simply to highlight the problem, or do you expect some kind of response from the audience?
- Define the problem (including, as far as possible, all relevant background and 'historical' information).
- Describe *significant* effects of the problem – who and/or what it affects, how the problem makes itself felt, etc.
- What possible/probable consequences may arise from
  - leaving the problem alone?
  - attacking it?

As appropriate:

- Call for suggestions.
- Describe solution(s).
- Recommend preferred solution (and say why it is preferred).
- Call for decision as to which solution is to be implemented/what further action is to be taken.

- Summarise the main points of the presentation and the discussion, and (where a decision has been reached) indicate what further action will be taken.

Now hear this

The final type of presentation is one designed simply to pass on information – to report progress in a certain area of the company's activities, or just promote general awareness.

Just as all presentations require a degree of salesmanship, they also aim to communicate some kind of information. In this particular type of presentation, however, this is the *primary* aim, with no secondary purpose. The presentation will normally contain the following elements:

- Introduction. Explain what the presentation is about, and what's in it for the members of the audience.
- Background information that will give the new material a context that makes sense to the audience. This will make the presentation more enjoyable and the new information more memorable.
- A clear and simple description of the new information to provide the framework that will make it as easy as possible for the audience to accept and absorb the data.
- A second review of the information, but this time with supporting evidence/details such as:
  - facts;
  - examples (as close as possible to the audience's area of experience);
  - comparisons;
  - statistics (but keep them simple);
  - expert opinions (where appropriate).
- Summarise the information, showing how it affects the members of the audience. If the company is moving into new markets, will this mean more work? More money? Greater job security? Show the *whole* picture.

Cutting your cloth

These five presentation outlines are designed to:

- gather opinions;
- publicise an idea or situation;
- sell an idea or course of action;
- highlight a problem (and seek a solution);
- pass on information.

They should be treated as simple templates which can be adapted to fit particular needs and situations. Feel free to pull them about and change them round. Always aim to create presentations in a way that will meet the needs of your audience and which you feel comfortable with. When you feel that a presentation is really *yours*, that's when your audience will perceive that you are in control of your material. This in turn will make them more inclined to accept whatever ideas, plans or information you set before them.

As a practical exercise you might want to scan through the chapter again with the following thought in mind:

> **Vivian has been asked to do a presentation on a new business opportunity, including a training element, so that members of staff can start to work on it within the next few days.**
> - **What elements should she include in her presentation?**
> - **Should the material be split into two separate presentations?**
> - **What would you do?**
> - **What factors would influence your decision?**

6

Know your audience

Putting the customer first

If there was ever a time for 'putting the customer first', it must be when you are preparing a presentation.

> Ken, from R&D, has to brief the sales team on any new products which his company plans to bring onto the market. Ken hates doing presentations and keeps them as short as possible. He makes very few notes and gets one of the secretaries to make up his foils.
>
> The foils are so detailed they are unreadable from more than three feet away. Nevertheless, Ken shows each foil for about 20 seconds (with a brief, jargon-laden explanation of each), there are no handouts, and Ken does his best to avoid any and all questions.

Strictly speaking, Ken does include all of the information that the sales team needs to know about the new products. But as exercises in communication, his briefings are a total flop. Because Ken hasn't given a second's thought for the people he is supposed to be communicating *with*. The sales people would be better off with an audiotape and copies of the foils that they could study at their leisure.

To stage a good presentation it is vital that you concentrate on the basic characteristics of your audience:

- Who will be attending the presentation, and what is their level of seniority/importance?
- Who is the decision maker (where relevant)?
- Is there any point in giving the presentation if certain people are unable to attend?
- Will people be attending your presentation by choice?
- Is their initial attitude likely to be pro, neutral or anti?
- How intelligent are they? Never talk down to people.
- How well informed are they? Will they have any background knowledge at all and, if so, how much?
- Will they understand any jargon you normally use?
- What sort of mood will they be in?
- What will they be expecting from you?
- How can you present your material so as to encourage a positive response (and avoid a negative reaction)?

The more accurately you can gauge these factors, and tailor your presentation accordingly, the more effective your communication will be.

Will they hear what you mean?

Do people automatically understand every word you say? No such luck!

In real life there is always a 'communication gap' – the

difference between what I meant to say, what I *actually* said, what you *think* you heard and what you *think* I meant.

This gap is particularly important when you are delivering a presentation. After all, the word 'audience' is a *collective* noun. It appears to be singular, but it is actually shorthand for 'an audience of individual listeners'.

And not just individuals, but individuals who have a wide variety of views on just about any topic you care to mention.

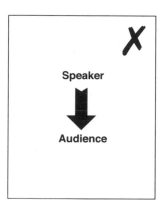 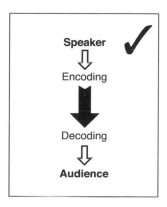

The communication gap

Here is a practical example of this gap:

Yesterday I watched a child playing with a dog.

What could be more straightforward than this simple sentence? The moment you read those words you understood exactly what they meant – didn't you? Are you sure about that?

Can *you* decode the sentence and answer these questions:

- **Was the child a little boy or a little girl?**
- **What age was the child?**
- **Where did this event take place?**
- **At what time of day did the event occur?**
- **What type of dog was the child playing with?**

- **What colour was the dog?**
- **Was the dog happy to play with the child?**
- **Why was I watching the child and the dog – was it my child, or my dog, or both, or neither?**

Although we can usually communicate quite easily without cross-checking every word, phrase and sentence, this example shows how much we take language for granted.

As Michael McCasky wrote in the *Harvard Business Review* over 30 years ago:

Another major point about the verbal environment of managers is that words are symbols, the meanings of which can vary greatly depending on who is using them. The point is troublesome, because it seems so obvious and at the same time contradicts an assumption we usually make in our everyday behavior. I have talked with managers who assume that words are entities and that communicating with another is essentially a process of logically ordering those entities. They direct all their effort toward getting the words right and presenting a logically structured train of thought in order to persuade.

As you examine misunderstandings between two managers, you will often find that what fouls the channels of communication is their mutual assumption that they are using the same words to mean the same things.

Vague and precise language

But if language tends to be so imprecise, knowing how to use it skilfully – knowing when to be vague and when to be precise, and how to do this without 'telegraphing' it to your audience – can be a valuable addition to any presenter's 'toolkit'. Five of the key factors which identify 'vague' language are:

- **Undefined nouns**
  What is missing in this undertaking: 'If necessary we will provide transport'? What's missing is a definition of the word 'transport'. Does it mean a hire car, a lorry, a bicycle or a pogo stick?
- **Undefined verbs**
  The same principle applies if you get an instruction such as: 'We want you to come to London.' *How* are you supposed to 'come to London'? By plane, by train, by car or on foot? And incidentally, who will be paying for this trip?
- **Undefined comparisons**
  'Our new product is bigger and better.' But 'bigger' and 'better' than what? Even the apparently more precise 'Our new product is now the best on the market' leaves several important questions unanswered: 'best' as measured by what criteria? What market, precisely? And so on.
- **Unsubstantiated rules**
  'We have to do it this way.' Why? Just because you've always done it that way before? What will happen if you use a different approach? Does it have to be done 'this way' even if 'this way' doesn't work?
- **Unattributed quotes**
  'All the research shows...', 'There was a study that came out last year...'. Who were these researchers? Who did the study, and working to what guidelines? Was the research really directly related to the subject being discussed?

It is all too easy to attach our own meanings to other people's words and then assume that they actually meant what we think they meant. This makes it especially important that we do whatever we can to make sure that when we're answering questions, we really understand what is being asked of us.

You may also want to check your own scripts or notes to see whether the degree of precision in your language is appropriate to your purpose.

In some situations, such as technical training, you may want to be very clear about what you mean. A sentence such as:

> Then you take the one you've got left and put it over by the one you did earlier.

though it may make perfect sense to you is unlikely to convey the same meaning to your audience as:

> Then, using both hands, carefully lift the red and black tube, with the cap pointing up so no liquid can leak out, and place it in the empty slot immediately to the left of the green and white striped tube that you prepared in the last session this morning.

If, on the other hand, you wanted to encourage some creativity on the part of your audience – when solving a problem in a team building exercise or brainstorming a name for a new product, for example – then you might deliberately make your language as vague as possible when describing the assignment, in order to give full rein to their powers of imagination.

Three learning/convincing styles

Every presentation involves some degree of learning, and while you cannot test for the learning mode of every person in the audience, you can at least be aware of, and work to, the three basic learning styles:

- **Show me.**
- **Tell me.**
- **Let me try it myself.**

(A fourth style, 'Let me read about it' is actually a variation on 'Show me', where the person is content to read about something rather than needing to see it firsthand. This last style occurs quite seldom, however, especially as compared with 'Show me,' which tends to be the most frequently used approach.)

These styles are, I must emphasise, context specific. People may tend to use one style more than the other two as a general rule, but we really are talking about *styles of learning* rather than 'Show me' people, 'Tell me' people, and so on.

These learning styles are in turn linked to, and explained by what are known as 'convincer channels' – the kinds of evidence we find persuasive or *convincing* rather than simply interesting or even 'not really very helpful'.

According to various studies, we can effectively recall:

- **20 per cent of what we hear;**
- **30 per cent of what we see;**
- **50 per cent of what we hear *and* see;**
- **70 per cent of what we do.**

Again the message is clear: for an effective event the audience should be able to see, hear and interact with the presenter and the presentation material.

- *Tell them* **what they *need* to know;**
- *Show them* **as much as is necessary to clarify, support and enhance your verbal message;**
- **Create opportunities for *interaction* – and that means more than just allowing time for questions.**

Some people find that they can work on all three elements of a presentation at the same time, whilst others find it easier to write the text, then design the visual component, then plan the points of interaction. Generally speaking, the first option is better insofar as it is less likely to produce a presentation that looks terrific but doesn't make much sense to anyone but the presenter. You might want to experiment to find out which method works best for you.

Audiences have feelings, too

It is always useful, as you prepare a presentation, to consider how it will come across to your audience by asking yourself how they might answer the following questions:

- **Did you feel that you were being *coerced*, or *persuaded*?**
- **Did you feel that you were being *guided*, or *manipulated*?**
- **Did you feel *motivated*, passive, or even *uninvolved*?**
- **Did the presenter successfully create rapport with the audience?**
- **Did you feel that there was *any* kind of interaction between the presenter and yourself?**
- **Did you feel that the presenter gave too much or too little *information*, or just the right amount?**
- **Was there an adequate opportunity to ask questions?**
- **Did members of the audience get full and relevant answers to their questions?**

Only when you are sure that you have addressed these considerations satisfactorily can you begin to feel that you have the basis for an effective presentation.

Incidentally, when it comes to modelling other presenters, this is a good basic checklist of things to look out for, taking account not only of *what* the presenter does, but also *how* they do it.

7

Words, words, words

The sweet KISS of success

For every thousand presentations that go on too long, only one or two will be too short. Very few presentations are literally *too short* (in terms of minutes and seconds), which gives a clue to the next secret of producing good presentations:

KISS

In its polite form this stands for **Keep It S**hort and **S**imple.

Mike Weatherley, one of the producers of the BBC TV programme *Business Matters*, is on record as saying: 'When I'm making a programme, I usually work on the basis that I can get three main points over in the programme.' The fact that a professional TV crew with all the hi-tech equipment and years of expertise at their disposal can't get more than three points across in half an hour is surely a lesson for anyone planning a presentation, no matter how sophisticated their set-up.

As basic guidelines:

- In 20 minutes (including the introduction and the conclusion) you have time for only *two* major point.
- In 30 minutes you might make *three* major points.
- In 40–45 minutes you *might* be able to cover *four* major points, but three points and a longer time for questions would be a better alternative.

Something to think about

Most adults have an attention span of somewhere between 25 and 40 minutes, and can only process five to nine chunks of information at any given time. Thus a presentation which contains too much information can be too long, even if it lasts for only 15–20 minutes. And if you speak for more than 45 minutes, it really doesn't matter how many points you make – unless they've taken notes or you have provided a handout most members of the audience will forget almost everything you say within the first couple of hours after you finish speaking!

You need to have the right amount of content, in a reasonable time span, delivered at an acceptable pace.

It's all in the timing

People come to a presentation to gain information which will be useful to them in some way. They come to *learn*, and they need time to *absorb* the new information. Without that time the information won't get past what is called *short-term memory*, and will soon be lost.

The lower line in the next diagram shows how increasing loss of concentration during the middle part of a presentation is directly related to the length of the presentation. Only the opening (*primary*) and closing (most *recent*) sections are retained to any great extent, and the recovery of attention towards the end of a presentation becomes smaller and smaller, the longer the session goes on.

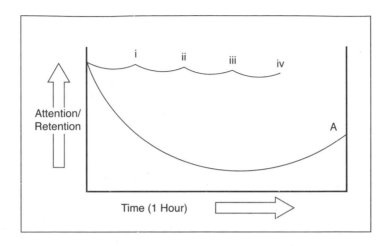

The upper, wavy line shows the effectiveness of the same material – properly structured – when the presentation is kept to a *maximum* running time of no more than 40 minutes. It really consists of several 'mini-presentations', each with its own lead in and climax. The 'peaks' are built-in *high spots* at 10, 20, and 30 minutes, which actively refocus audience attention, making it easier to maintain concentration *between* the peak points.

Waving or drowning?

By the way, when you use this 'mini-presentation' approach it is important to let your audience know what's going on, rather than expecting them to understand it all by themselves. After all, if you are dividing your presentation into distinct sections but don't have appropriate 'signposts' along the way then someone in your audience who loses concentration for just a minute or so at the wrong moment may refocus on what you are saying, find it has no direct reference to what you were saying a minute or two ago, and remain thoroughly confused at precisely the moment when you need them to be understanding exactly what you are telling them.

The solution is to treat each mini-presentation as though it was a presentation in its own right, with a brief introduction, a coherent internal structure and a closing summary.

Thus the initial introduction should preview the entire presentation ('tell them what you're going to tell them'), whilst subsequent introductions should only link the new section to the previous section. Likewise the final summary should draw together everything in the entire presentation, but intermediate summaries should only deal with the material in the section you've just completed.

In practice the summary and introduction between sections work best when the summary runs into the introduction, something like this:

> So, those are the five reasons why I think we need to take action [briefly list the five reasons]. Is everyone clear about that? [The question is optional, of course, offering you the chance to clear up any misunderstandings before you carry on.] Now, with those reasons in mind I'd like to look at the three courses of action that are open to us...

If you are using a projector or a flipchart you might want to have a foil of the summary points for each section, or have them pre-written on a page of your flipchart.

On confronting a blank sheet of paper

A blank sheet of paper that must be filled is one of the most daunting objects known to man, so:

> Don't start with a blank sheet of paper.

Yes, I'm serious. I've used this process for years, it is highly efficient and can be learned in a matter of minutes!

The one-man think tank

All you need for this technique is a sheet of plain paper (A4 is OK; A3 size is better), plus a set of coloured pens or pencils.

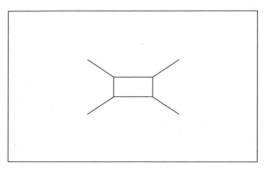

Lay the paper down with one of the long sides towards you and draw a rectangular box in the centre of the page with a line at each corner. (If possible draw the central box and the four lines radiating from it in different colours.)

You will immediately notice the difference between this approach and drawing up a list of the topics to be covered, which can easily end up as nothing but a censored series of ideas – in no particular order (see below left):

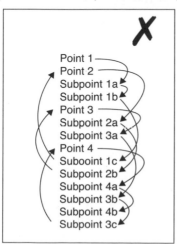

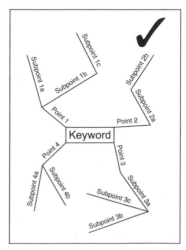

Even if we try to impose some order upon the list – by drawing in linking lines, for example – the end result is often even more confused than before and still gives only a vague idea of the relationships *between* points. The spidergram (above right), on the other hand, clearly illustrates individual points and the overall structure. What can only be *inferred* from the linked list is made patently obvious in the spidergram.

Incidentally, as far as setting out your spidergram is concerned, the following guidelines are recommended:

- **The 'keyword' in the central box should be a one or two word abbreviation of your primary objective.**
- **Use just one or two words on each 'limb', even a whole phrase if necessary – but never a complete sentence.**
- **Use the full range of colours you have available.**
- **If different parts of the spidergram seem to link up, indicate this fact with a linking arrow rather than duplicating a whole set of 'limbs'.**

Once you have completed your spidergram you may need to do some serious pruning to bring it back to three main points. It will help to go back to your statement of objectives and start cutting out those parts of your diagram which aren't directly relevant to your primary purpose.

Creating a structure

Having assembled your ideas, the next step is to give them some structure so that the members of your audience get a clear understanding of the points you are making *as you go along*.

All too often novice presenters take the order in which they had their ideas and use that as the structure for the actual presentation. Sometimes, if they're very lucky, it works. Most times it doesn't, and the presentation is peppered with phrases like 'which I will explain later on' and 'I'd like to add some comments to something I said earlier about...'

One very effective way to create a structure for your presentation is to take the main points you plotted on your spidergram and write each of them on a separate file card or Post-it® note. Then shuffle the individual sections around until you have what seems like a coherent sequence.

Next try reading through the sections aloud, preferably into a tape recorder, bearing in mind factors such as:

- **Have I introduced the subject clearly and in such a way that everyone will understand what the presentation is about and what they're expected to get from it?**
- **Does the presentation follow a clear sequence from start to finish? Have I made sure that I introduce each sub-topic before I start to talk about it – 'B will depend on A, which I described earlier...' is far better than 'Of course, B will depend on A, and I'll tell you more about A in just a minute...'**
- **Have you broken the information down into 'digestible' chunks of a size likely to suit the existing knowledge level of your audience?**
- **Do your closing remarks genuinely wrap the presentation up and show how everything fits together?**

Repeat this process, if necessary, until you are satisfied that your presentation meets all of these requirements.

All the truth that's fit to present

People tend to respond more readily to upbeat presentations, so concentrate on the *positive* elements of what you want to say and the *negative* aspects of any contrary information. There is nothing wrong in presenting your case in the best possible light so long as you don't use distortions or lies.

Having said that, you must also allow for people's natural cynicism. If you paint too rosy a picture avoiding *all* contrary evidence, your audience may become more than a little suspicious. You can actually strengthen your case by including one or two possible objections – which you then demolish – rather than trying to pretend that no objections exist.

Think ahead – plan ahead

Once you think that your basic script is complete, run through it with these three considerations in mind:

- **Have you said everything you need to say?**
- **Have you said too much?**
- **Have you left any obvious hooks for questions?**

If necessary, you can now edit your script to resolve any obviously outstanding questions or ambiguous statements, and to remove any 'loose ends'.

You can also script answers to questions that might be asked but which you don't want to cover in the presentation.

Script, notes or cue cards?

It usually takes me more than three weeks to prepare a good impromptu speech.

Mark Twain

I once asked a particularly impressive speaker how long it had taken to develop such an effortless, flowing style. The gentleman concerned led me on stage and pointed to the top of the lectern, and some 20 cue cards.

'No one can give a good presentation without doing the preparation,' he told me. 'And very few people are skilled enough to work without some kind of notes.

'What you get from experience isn't the ability to skip the groundwork – it's the facility to make it look like you didn't have to do the groundwork!'

So, which *physical* format is most suitable for your text?

Clearly, your presentation style should match your current level of expertise. How good is your memory under pressure, for example? It may look very professional if you appear to be speaking 'off the cuff', but how professional will it look if you say 'Next Monday' when you mean 'A week on Monday', or if you say '27 per cent' when you should have said '72 per cent'?

Some people really can produce a speech at the drop of a hat. Most of us need some form of script.

Full script

A full script takes time to prepare since it must be more or less word perfect. If you don't happen to have a professional scriptwriter on hand, you may have to produce several drafts before you get your script worded entirely to your satisfaction.

Using a full script can be a great confidence builder. You cannot forget your lines; there is no danger of leaving something unsaid or of giving out incorrect information; and you can time your presentation with considerable accuracy.

On the minus side, it is exceedingly difficult to write a script that sounds natural, let alone read a script so that it sounds natural. You must constantly break eye contact in order to look down at your script, and you are more or less tied to the lectern or whatever your notes are resting on.

> **Tip:**
> Modularise your script.
>   Write it so that you can add or remove material in neat chunks if the need arises.

A word-for-word text is also notoriously inflexible. If any part of your script needs to be changed at the last moment you'll just have to cross out the obsolete material and make do with what is left – or learn to write very fast!

Notes

It is not unknown for a speaker to use a spidergram as the 'notes' for a presentation. It is more common, however, to prepare notes with main headings, sub-headings, and a brief outline of each point that you wish to make. In short, a rough guide to what you want to say.

Using notes means that you have something down in black and white (for confidence building), and in a format that can easily be edited right up to the last moment. If time runs short you can use the same material, but simply deal with each point in less detail.

Notes also allow you to *appear* more spontaneous, since you really will be speaking 'off the cuff', to a certain extent.

The main drawback to using notes is that it is entirely up to you to have to *remember* what you meant to say about each heading or sub-heading. You will also need a place where you can rest your notes so that you can see them, but the audience can't.

Cue cards

Since cue cards (for example, box file cards, approximately 10 centimetres by 15 centimetres) are much smaller than A4 sheets of paper, you will need to work with key words and phrases rather than sentences.

Tip:

To avoid getting your cue cards mixed up, number them distinctly in one corner. Or punch a hole in one corner of each card so that they can be held together by a treasury tag or similar fastening.

Using cue cards means that you can carry part of your script with you if you want to move away from the lectern. This will give you virtually unlimited freedom of movement.

The downside of using cue cards is the lack of written information, because all of the cards for your presentation should fit easily into a jacket pocket or handbag. If they don't, your presentation may be too long, or you're putting too much on your cue cards. Perhaps you should be using notes?

Visual aids as memory joggers

Using the visual aids as an abbreviated script cuts down on preparation and allows a great deal of flexibility. But you will need to check each visual as you display it, which could mean that you spend more time looking at the displays than at the audience. You should also avoid making the visual aids more detailed to compensate for the lack of script or notes.

Foil backing sheets

If you have foils with backing sheets, these can be used:

- **to carry a copy of the contents of the foil;**
- **for notes regarding the contents of the foil.**

As your presentations skills develop you may find that this is a practical alternative to the options suggested above.

If the cap fits

So the real answer as to how you should prepare your script is: it's really up to you.

Try each of the styles – full script, notes, cue cards or memory joggers – and see which works best for you.

When you come to the end – stop

The intro and the outro

The two parts of your presentation that will be remembered most clearly are the start and the finish – especially the finish. A good ending may turn a rather mediocre presentation into a success. Likewise, a bad ending can ruin an otherwise excellent presentation, leaving the audience feeling dissatisfied and critical rather than impressed and appreciative.

Always aim to finish a presentation (no matter what the subject) on a positive note. Give your delegates something to take away that they can build on so that the presentation becomes an ongoing experience.

This will be much easier to achieve if you adhere to the rule that every presentation needs a clear, well-planned *purpose*.

What was it all about?

As we've already seen, the purpose or outcome of a presentation is the foundation stone of the whole structure. The closing section of a presentation is the final and equally vital part of that structure, and must be something more than just the end of the event. It must summarise all that has gone before and create a bridge to whatever happens next.

What your audience will really need to know is:

- **What** (are we supposed to do)?
- **When** (do we do it)?
- **How** (will we know when we've done it satisfactorily)?

Your closing remarks should answer those questions as precisely and clearly as possible.

Closing comments

One of the most common reasons for lost sales is not that the sales person has made a bad sales pitch, but rather that they didn't close the sale. That is, after describing and demonstrating all the advantages of their product, they forgot to ask that crucial last question: 'How many would you like?' or 'Will you be paying with cash, a cheque or a credit card?'

Many presentations also fail because the presenter hasn't 'closed' in an appropriate manner. Three common errors that occur at the end of a presentation are:

The emergency stop

Without a hint of warning the speaker pulls up, in a metaphorical screech of brakes, with a phrase such as:

Well, I think that's all I have to say, so I'll stop there.

The speaker 'thinks' that they have nothing more to say? Didn't they draw up some kind of script? Don't they *know* that they: have nothing more to say? Maybe they've left something out, but how will we ever know?

By the time you come to the end of a presentation, you should have answered the three vital questions What? When? and How? and there should be no need to announce the fact. Nor is it necessary to offer a self-evident observation such as: 'I've finished so I'll stop.'

If you *have* finished, unexpectedly or not, leave it at that and either invite questions or sit down, depending on how the event has been arranged.

The endless maze

The 'endless maze' speaker can be recognised by the way that they end up as lost and confused as their audience, thus:

> And so I'll finish on that point – and remind you of the comment I made earlier about...

And off they go again.

It's as though they are lost in some kind of oral maze, frequently sighting the exit but never quite able to reach it before veering off down another detour.

This speaker presumably isn't working from a well-prepared script or they would have no trouble reaching the exit. This gives the impression that they simply threw a few major headings together in a hurry, and now they're hoping that if they talk for long enough they are bound to cover all the finer (unscripted) details, sooner or later.

The clichéd climax

Unlike the 'emergency stop', where the speaker seems to arrive at an ending by accident, the 'clichéd climax' presenter obviously knows exactly when they are going to finish – and insist on broadcasting the fact:

In conclusion...
Just before I close...
And finally...
I'd like to leave you with this thought...

as though preparing us for that terrible moment when they stop speaking and all the joy will go out of our lives.

The more the merrier

All of these examples clearly illustrate the need for a well-ordered structure in any presentation. Not just because it seems like a good idea, but because it saves so much trouble in the long run – as in the case of the 'more the merrier' ending.

Favourite phrases this time include:

And in addition...
I'd also like to say/point out/remind you...

Unlike the 'endless maze', (where the speaker keeps returning to earlier comments) for a 'more the merrier' speaker the end is not the end after all, but a new beginning. The process of summing up their ideas seems to generate a whole series of new thoughts. The audience, on the other hand, will only remain attentive for a limited amount of time.

Last-minute ideas, no matter how brilliant, should be saved for another day unless they genuinely dovetail into the points set out in your script – and are essential to the effectiveness of the presentation.

Know when to stop

Speakers often find themselves in 'endless maze' or 'more the merrier' mode through finishing ahead of time – and thereby snatch defeat from the very jaws of success.

In reality, few presentations fail by ending early – unless the premature ending is due to lack of adequate preparation. If you can say everything you need to say in less than your allotted time that is a bonus, not an error. Don't spoil the effect by trying to pad your speech up to the 'official' length. Make the most of the situation by allowing an extended question and answer session or by inserting an extra comfort break.

Happy endings

Having described some 'presentation pitfalls', let's move on now to get some ideas on how it should be done.

The closing summary

A closing summary, though useful in almost any setting, is most suitable in a presentation that is only intended to communicate information and doesn't require any follow-up activity by the members of the audience. Carefully avoiding clichés such as:

> So, before I finish I'd just like to summarise the points we've covered this afternoon...

you can proceed straight into the summary with no introduction at all after your last key point, as in:

> So, we've seen what kind of pressures the company faces [*list the pressures*], and the possible ways in which those pressures can be handled [*list the alternatives*]...

The challenge

Issuing a challenge to the audience is used to best effect where a particular problem has been addressed, or where you are calling for greater or renewed effort.

Couch the challenge in terms of what 'we can' do, or 'we will' do, and state a precise course of action in this context. A mere emotional appeal for some (unspecified) action may be very rousing at the time, but it is likely to lead to confusion and/ or apathy when the members of the audience actually try to put your rhetoric into practice.

The 'call to action'

When the intended result is to generate agreement on a particular course of action, it may be more effective to use persuasion rather than a challenge. On this basis it is valid to confine your summation to the points in favour of the proposed action and to end by stating precisely what the next step should be.

Since you will presumably have covered any contradictory arguments – and answered them – in the course of your presentation, it is unnecessary to state them all over again.

One outstanding example of a *call to action* came as the climax of a political rally, when the party leader exhorted his followers to: 'Go home and prepare to rule!'

As it turned out, the call was somewhat over optimistic. No matter. Its purpose was to grab newspaper headlines and create a positive attitude in the conference hall. In both respects it was hugely successful.

The 'feel good' factor

Motivational speakers aim to leave the audience with a warm glow rather than indicating some further course of action. This would work well in the closing session of a multi-presentation event where you wish to reinforce the group identity, for example, but would definitely be out of place at a relatively impersonal event such as a press conference.

Two popular forms of the 'feel good' ending make use of

a quotation or a piece of poetry respectively. In both cases the material should be short and to the point, though the 'point' in question does not have to be directly linked to the subject of the presentation. As long as the material is highly emotionally charged, the contents of the quotation or poem will depend on the emotional response you want to arouse in your audience, rather than by the subject of the presentation.

Beware the red light

If you've ever watched an event where the coloured lights are used to signal to speakers when their time is up you may also have noticed how often speakers start to panic when the amber light comes on, though they surely know how long they could speak for when they were preparing their speech.

There are times, of course, when audience reactions last longer than the speaker expected, which has thrown their timing out. Thus a well-prepared speaker always arms themself with two copies of their closing comments.

One copy is based on the assumption that nothing unforeseen will happen, and the speaker will have all the time that they need to wrap up the presentation at their own speed. The second copy, (the copy that so many speakers overlook) is set out on the basis that everything that *can* go wrong *will* go wrong and that they will need to wind up their comments in very short order indeed.

The length of the 'emergency' ending will depend on the length of the presentation as a whole. If your entire speech lasts only 5 or 10 minutes then allow one or two minutes for your long ending, and 30–45 seconds for the emergency ending (that's about 60–90 words at a normal speaking pace). If your presentation is scheduled for mor e than 30 minutes the two endings would be longer – but not too much longer.

9

Curtain up!

On your marks, get set...

Before we get into the main issues covered in this chapter I'd like to address the question: when should you start?

Let's say your presentation, or the next session of the seminar/course/conference/meeting, etc, is due to start at 3.30 pm – but when it comes to 3.30 you know that several people still aren't in the room. Do you start anyway or do you wait for everyone to arrive? To be honest, there is no single answer – but here are some ideas you might like to consider:

- **The person still missing is the person who will have to make the decision the presentation is all about.**
  If the material you are about to cover must be heard by one or more people who have not yet arrived then you really don't have any choice but to wait.

  This may be frustrating, especially if this is a sales presentation, but there's obviously no point in going on until all of the key people are present. The only

consolation is that everyone else having to wait with you will understand the predicament you are in.

- You are dealing with an 'audience of equals' – on a training course, for example – and one or more people don't show up on time.

  In this situation you should always aim to start on time even if half the seats are still empty. To do otherwise is an insult to the people who bothered to be there on time and wrecks your timetable so that you have to simplify your material or even miss stuff out altogether, and it also carries the message to those who are missing that they really don't need to take any notice when you announce the starting time of a session, because in practice you are willing to stand around just waiting for them to turn up. Now they control the presentation, not you.

- You have decided to wait – for whatever reason. What do you do next? Starting today, you need to develop a set of 'ice-breakers' and other such exercises that can also be adapted as time fillers with a practical purpose. That way, any time you want to wait for latecomers to arrive (after all, they may have been held up for some entirely genuine and unavoidable reason), you can put the time to a practical purpose.

  Strictly speaking, 'ice-breakers' are usually used to get people to get to know each other at the start of a course, etc. If you're part way through a course or seminar then the most obvious exercise is to get the members of your audience to divide up into groups of three, four or five (depending on the overall size of the audience – larger audience, means larger groups), then have them discuss either what went on in the previous session, or the event as a whole, or what they hope to get out of the next session, etc.

The moment you walk in the joint...

And now, back to the subject of first impressions.

Within 5–10 *seconds* of your entrance, every member of your audience will have formed a subconscious opinion of you. These 'first impressions' will colour how your audience perceive the presentation as a whole.

According to a series of experiments carried out by psychologist Professor Robert Rosenthal, and others, people can rate a presenter or teacher on characteristics such as happy/depressed, confident/anxious and so on with nearly 70 per cent accuracy after seeing the person in action for as little as 10 seconds, as compared with ratings by people who had seen that person in action over a period of 2–3 months.

So whilst your audience may take note of a lot more than 7 per cent of what you say, their impression of you – your public image, so to speak – owes a great deal more to how you look and sound rather than to what you say. You quite literally have to be able to 'walk the talk'.

Not surprisingly, then, it is estimated that the overall impact of a presentation will be enhanced by anything up to 18 or 20 per cent by a well-judged introduction. It must first act as a 'hook' to catch your audience's attention, and then go on to:

- **create a framework;**
- **set the mood;**
- **create motivation;**
- **establish your credibility;**
- **summarise your message;**
- **indicate whether batteries are included;**
- **set out your time lines.**

Let's start, then, by looking at some of the different ways in which you can bait that 'hook'.

Quotations

There are a number of excellent books of quotations on the market, but be sure to select a quote that is appropriate, and from someone who will have credibility with your audience:

> 'As Winston Churchill once said...'
> 'As Mabel Ramsbotham once observed...'

Most people have at least a vague idea that Winston Churchill was someone famous and important. But who cares what Mabel Ramsbotham once observed? Unless, of course, she is a well-respected colleague, a department head or the managing director, in which case her opinion may well count for a lot more than the thoughts of Winston Churchill.

Humour

There are two basic forms of humour – *instinctive* and *deliberate*. Instinctive humour grows out of whatever happens during the presentation material – the sort of humour that 'you had to be there to appreciate'.

Deliberate humour, on the other hand, encompasses jokes, funny stories, cartoons and so on. If you're seriously considering using 'deliberate' humour in your presentation, I suggest that you think long and hard – and then change your mind. One *relevant* story will work far better than half a dozen jokes.

The important questions to ask yourself about any kind of humour are:

- **Will people understand it (as you intended it)?**
- **Will they find it funny?**

If you're not sure on either count, try something else.

Questions

Asking a question right at the start of a presentation is a good way of letting your audience know that you wish to communicate *with* them, rather than simply lecture *at* them.

For the best effect ask the audience a question that only allows for an unqualified 'Yes/No' answer (preferably 'Yes'), such as 'Can you hear me at the back?'

Also make sure that you are asking for a manageable response. The question: 'Is the seating comfortable?' is certainly relevant. But what do you do if a majority of the audience answer 'No'?

Visual impact

You could wait until everyone is seated, then leap on to the stage wearing a gorilla suit and waving a bunch of bananas. Or then again, maybe not.

Whilst fashions in general are becoming more relaxed, many people still believe that 'clothes make the man – or woman', and they will happily judge you on your physical appearance. If you want people to take notice of what you have to *say*, dress to meet your audience's expectations.

The classic 'power outfit' for men is a dark suit, white shirt, a conservatively patterned tie with plenty of crimson or scarlet (not pillar box red!). Socks should be plain navy blue or black. Shoes should be black, in good repair and well polished. (Judging a man by the state of his shoes is far more common in business circles than you might imagine.)

For women, changing attitudes mean that it is no longer necessary to wear a female version of the male power outfit described above. 'Classic' outfits, such as a blazer or collarless jacket with a skirt, trouser suits and dresses, are all acceptable. Colour schemes should be sober (though not sombre), and chosen to complement individual hair, eye and skin coloration. Items to avoid include lacy tops, floppy collars, conspicuous jewellery and scarves which need constant adjustment.

By the way, if the presentation is anything but a formal business event, there is chance that people might not know what kind of clothes *they* should wear (formal business suit, smart casual or whatever)? It can save a lot of embarrassment if you specify the correct dress code in the invitation to the presentation.

Topical references

Topical references can be used to great effect, as long as they are genuinely relevant to the subject under discussion – and everyone knows what you're talking about.

Personal anecdotes

These must be *very* appropriate, and brief, to justify their use. I still remember an event from quite some time ago, where the speaker opened his presentation with a personal anecdote that started: 'You know, I nearly didn't live long enough to make this presentation...'

At that moment he had the unqualified attention of everyone in the room. By the time he struggled to the end of the story, some three or four minutes later, most people in the audience were thinking, 'So what?'

Shocking statistics

If you want to use a shocking statistic – to get your audience's attention without actually insulting them – then make it as simple but as hard-hitting as possible. Something like:

> Seventy-five per cent of all retired people are living on a greatly reduced income. Thirty per cent of all retired people are living on or below the poverty line.
>
> *[Short pause]*
>
> The material we're going to cover in this presentation could save you becoming a part of those statistics!

Used well, shocking statistics can be extremely effective, as long as you remember that statistics are easily misunderstood, unless the information is kept short and simple.

Outrageous statements

> Speaker (*to audience of computer programmers*): 'Do you realise that you are wasting your time if you don't have a competent technical author to prepare your documentation?'
>
> *[Short pause]*
>
> 'At least, that's how your customers may see it.'

From the audience's point of view this was definitely a highly contentious opening, but it achieved its purpose.

The 'outrageous statement' opening will undoubtedly make your audience sit up and take notice, and if it (gently) ruffles a few feathers it may also help the audience to remember the message when a more 'gentlemanly', neutral presentation has long since faded from memory.

Teasers

One trainer I used to work with liked to have the following four instructions written up on a flipchart or whiteboard before the delegates started to arrive:

- **Make mistakes**
- **Ask 'dumb' questions**
- **Cheat**
- **Have fun**

Once the delegates were assembled he would explain that the four points meant:

- **Nobody is perfect, so understand that making mistakes is a valuable element in the learning process.**
- **If you don't understand something, say so, it's part of my job to make this as clear as I can.**
- **Forget everything you learned in school about not looking at other people's work. In business we work best when we pool our knowledge and our expertise.**
- **Treat this course as an opportunity, not as an obligation. The more you enjoy the course, the more effectively will you absorb the course material.**

Maps and shoehorns

Once your audience is satisfactorily 'hooked' there are other functions an introduction must serve.

In one situation you may want to calm and reassure your audience, whilst on another occasion it may be an essential part of the presentation that you get them stirred up and excited. In either case, one way of achieving the required result might be to 'draw a map' of the 'territory' you intend to cover.

This is also an effective way of dealing with a situation where you know that different members of the audience have quite different views on the main topic of the presentation. In this case, the purpose of the 'mapping' process is to provide a clear, definitive view of the topic. You can't expect everyone to fall in line with your definition automatically, of course, but at least it will be plain to all concerned just where the presentation is coming from – and where you plan to go.

Just how detailed your map needs to be will depend on whether the members of your audience have any (relevant) prior knowledge of the topic being discussed. In some situations, people may have nearly as much information as you have yourself, in which case it is simply a question of fleshing out that knowledge so that they can make a decision, undertake a particular course of action, or whatever.

If you find that your audience knows little or nothing about the subject of the presentation, then your initial map must be more detailed, providing them with the necessary background information.

Think of this rather like a shoehorn, easing your audience into the subject. Introduce some small part of your topic by relating it to something that the audience members will already know about and which matters to them. This will reassure them that your topic is comprehensible, and that the presentation is relevant to their current situation/ future needs. It will also give them the confidence to follow along, even if things get a little complicated and technical later on.

Setting a mood

How do you want your audience to feel as the presentation starts? Relaxed? Alert? Critical? Receptive?

Your opening remarks will play a crucial role in setting the mood of the whole presentation. Would you open a presentation with a shocking statistic or statement if you wanted the audience to feel relaxed and receptive? Would you try to stir your sales force to greater efforts by the use of soft lights and a 'fireside chat'?

For maximum effect you must analyse your audience as far as possible, and then make a best guess as to what kind of approach will produce the required response from that particular set of people. Above all, never assume that any two audiences will react the same way to the same material; they won't.

Creating motivation

To make people take notice of what you have to say, you must give them a reason to listen; a reason which relates to their own experience. In other words, you must answer their unspoken question, 'What's in it for me.'

This may seem rather mercenary but, as Dale Carnegie points out in *How to Win Friends and Influence People*, self-interest is an incredibly effective source of motivation.

So talk to your audience as they are, not as you would like them to be. This will benefit from as much audience analysis as you can manage. Some members of your audience may have been 'volunteered', but don't let this put you off. It may actually be easier to sell the presentation to those people if you can only show them that they aren't going to be wasting their time after all.

American social psychologist Abraham Maslow has described what might be called a *hierarchy of motivation*:

The pyramid represents various levels of achievement. Maslow argued that people can only be motivated to move up to the next level when they have satisfactorily met the basic requirements of their current level. You are unlikely to have much success encouraging a company to embark on a major reorganisation when their most pressing need is to find enough money to pay their suppliers!

For maximum effect, then, you must *engage* your audience's attention at their *current* level, and then show them how your presentation will fulfil their natural inclination to move up to the next level of motivation.

Establishing credibility

Establishing your credentials is a surprisingly delicate affair. A string of academic and/or professional qualifications, and details of your years as the right hand of God, may sound impressive, but you are far more likely to achieve rapport if you adopt a style of introduction that is more gentle on your audience's self-esteem.

Are batteries included?

Always let your audience know whether some kind of follow-up action will be expected of them, and how they can tell when they have successfully completed that action. The phrase 'Sales must rise' may sound like a clear objective at the time, yet it really doesn't say very much at all. Which sales must rise? How much must they rise by? Over what time period?

Making and breaking expectations

It is always a good move to show your audience that you are aware of their expectations, and to clear up any misconceptions that you know or believe exist regarding the reason(s) for the presentation. Get your audience to believe that you are all there for a common purpose and see how it builds rapport.

Providing a framework

People find it easier to absorb new information if they can relate it to the knowledge that they already possess – hence the repetitive nature of the guideline: tell them what you're going to tell them, tell them, and then, tell them what you've told them – (and why).

Wherever it is appropriate, always aim to use your introduction to create a bridge from the audience's existing knowledge to your *new* information.

By the way, though this three-step approach is often seen as something of a cliché, recent research has revealed that the human brain has a strategy for deciding what is important and what probably isn't, and what we need to be able to recall and what we can probably afford to 'forget'. And it all has to do with the 'rule of three', so to speak.

If I tell you something once, then, unless it is something quite remarkable or you can immediately recognise a direct relevance to yourself, there's a fair chance you will forget it after only a few hours – if that. If I tell you the same thing a second time – not immediately, but after about, say, 10 to 15 minutes – your brain will still remember the first time I told you and it will identify this as something that might turn out to be important. The information gets 'flagged', so to speak, but there's still quite a strong possibility that the information will be stored in a less-than-optimal manner. BUT, if I now tell you the same thing again after another 10 to 15 minutes (approximately), then your brain finally registers the fact that this really is important information and needs to be stored in such a way as to make it easy to recall.

Quite why the brain should attach any special importance to three statements of the same information is not clear, but this finding does at last make sense of the 'folk wisdom' advice to:

- **Tell them what you you're going to tell them.**
- **Tell them.**
- **Tell them what you've told them.**

Times and events

When several presentations follow on from one another, set people's minds at rest (and thereby make them more receptive) by reviewing the total situation, not just your part of it.

Some presenters talk through a foil listing events and times.

Or, you might include a timetable as part of the initial handout and then use a foil to confirm that everything will go as planned, or to explain any alterations to the programme.

By the way, when you say your presentation will last for 10, 20 or 30 minutes, don't let it go to 15, 25 or 35 minutes.

Never say not!

Human beings cannot think in negatives.

If I say to you: 'Don't think of a pig in a straw hat riding a bicycle', it's extremely likely that the very first thing you will do is think of a pig in a straw hat riding a bicycle – and quite naturally so. After all, how can you be sure that you aren't thinking about something, unless you first have a clear idea what it is that you're not going to think about?

Remember the fad for shifting the word 'not' to the end of a sentence to give a twist to the meaning of what had just been said? For example, 'He has a really great car – not!' That reflects how our brains actually work. The brain *hears* 'I don't mean to criticise' as 'I mean to criticise – not.' By the time it processes 'not' it has already heard you 'admit' that you're being critical!

If there's something you don't want the audience to think about – *leave it out*. If you say it, they'll think about it, no matter *how* carefully you phrase it.

10

Selecting and using visual aids

Just for effect?

Why use visual aids? Just consider the following statistics:

- We learn about 90% of what we know *visually* – from films, books, etc. Only 7–11% is learned through hearing alone.
- The average audience member will remember about 70% of a purely verbal presentation three hours later, and as little as 10% only three days later.
- Of a purely visual presentation, about 75% will be remembered after three hours, and up to 20% after three days.
- About 85% of a mixed verbal/visual presentation will be recalled after three hours, and as much as 66% will be remembered after three days.
- Presenters who use visual aids are generally perceived as being more professional and persuasive than those who rely on speech alone.

In short, for a truly powerful *and memorable* presentation you will need to include some form of visual aid.

Horses for courses

It has to be said, however, that visual aids can only be justified when used well. From the options available to you, think very carefully about which form of visual aid will best suit your purpose, your audience and your own skill.

(It is advisable to avoid using different kinds of visual aid simultaneously unless you have professional assistance – and plenty of practice.)

Chalkboard

Although 'Chalk and Talk' seems to be enjoying a new-found popularity at the moment, and whist this medium is certainly cheap, it is also extremely limited and really only suitable for small groups (a dozen or less), and where more modern facilities are not available (few presentation venues include the kind of huge 'boards' found in university lecture rooms).

Whiteboard and pen

Whilst a whiteboard is definitely one step up from a chalkboard, it still requires legible handwriting to be effective. If in doubt, stick to using capital letters. Whiteboards are suitable for informal meetings such as discussion groups and brainstorming, and for ad hoc displays in formal meetings (as an alternative to a flipchart). Audience size (maximum 20–30) will depend on the quality of your handwriting and the size of the board.

Tip:

As a rule of thumb, *always* put the cap back on a marker pen when you stop writing, to avoid having it dry out.

One of the main drawbacks of using a whiteboard is the lack of any permanent record of what was written/drawn on the board once it has been cleaned off, though electronic whiteboards are now available which will give an A4-sized printout of the current contents of the writing area.

Flipcharts

Flipcharts are portable and quite cheap – but can be a little hard to handle. They are suitable for multi-coloured displays, but some types of ink tend to 'bleed' through flipchart-type paper. Once again, the presenter's handwriting skills are an important factor. If you usually have to decipher your writing for other readers, avoid flipcharts.

Flipcharts can be used to great effect with groups of up to 30 people, especially when it is necessary to record lists of ideas or display 'spur of the moment' information.

Individual pages and sequences can be prepared in advance and/or built up as the presentation goes along, and pages can be torn off and stuck up on the wall with Blu-Tack to create an expanding display.

Tip:
1. To find pages easily in a set of pre-prepared flipchart pages, make a sticky tape tag for each page down the side of the chart where you usually stand.
2. If you know that you will have to draw a quite complicated chart or diagram during the presentation, lightly pencil it in beforehand, then simply follow the pencil lines.

Overhead projector (OHP)

The OHP has become one of the most widely used visual aids in business presentations. Given an adequate screen and appropriate seating arrangements it is suitable for almost any size of audience up to the low hundreds.

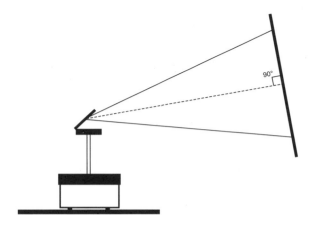

To get the best image with an OHP, the screen should, ideally, be at right angles to a line drawn from the centre of the screen to the centre of the projection mirror (see illustration). Thus a wall, even a plain white one, is *not* an entirely satisfactory alternative to a proper screen.

As a general rule, the size of screen for a given venue can be calculated using the ratio of 1:6; thus, if the last row of seats is 14 metres (42 feet) from the screen, the screen should be 14/6 = 2.3 metres square (42/6 = 7 feet square). Minimum screen size should be about 1.5 metres square (5 feet square).

Foils are a very flexible medium and are suitable for formal or informal presentations, especially where any type of graphical information is involved.

The main advantages of an OHP are its ease of use and the option of switching between various display styles. Foils may be used:

- In straight display mode where the entire foil is immediately visible.
- As a sequence of overlays, to build up a complex picture.
- In 'progressive revelation' fashion, whereby points are revealed one at a time by sliding a mask down the foil.

The main disadvantage of using an OHP is the difficulty of ensuring that everyone can see the whole screen, especially those people sitting in the first few rows:

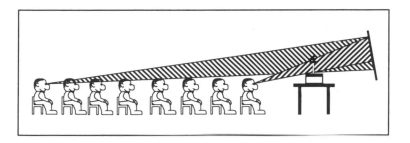

This situation is almost inevitable unless the OHP is correctly positioned on a purpose-built stand. It is the main reason why you should never use the whole area of an OHP foil.

- Text on an OHP foil should be *at least* 6–7 millimetres in height (that's between 24 pt and 28 pt), and will need to increase to about 15 millimetres (or 60 pt) if any part of the audience will be more than 14–16 metres (40–45 feet) away from the screen. (4 pts = 1 millimetre approx.)
- Always use foils in the 'landscape' position to minimise poor visibility, and leave a margin of at least 2.5 centimetres (1 inch) on all four sides of the foil. Do not use the bottom third of the foil at all if you can possibly avoid it.
- Ten to 12 words on each foil is a sensible maximum. If a foil is too 'busy', your audience will happily ignore what you are saying until they have read the foil all the way through – or until you move on to the next foil.

In the example above, the foil on the left actually contains four separate headings. The foil on the right shows the first heading set out correctly (the rest of the left-hand foil should have been divided to make three further foils, following the same basic guidelines).

Computer-based displays

There are three main ways of utilising computer-generated displays in a presentation context. A computer linked to:

> one or more large-screen TVs;
> a video projection package;
> or a tabletop projector.

When I first wrote about computer-based displays about 15 years ago, the most common options were TVs or video projectors. Since then the situation has changed radically with projectors getting ever smaller and cheaper and accepting multiple simultaneous connections to computers, VC players, and so on. In a well-equipped setting including multiple screens, it should be quite possible to cater for audiences of a hundred or more delegates. A computer-based display is now the method-of-choice for most situations – from a simple talk to a live demonstration of a piece of software for sales or training purposes, and it is limited only by the power of the projector.

Tip:
Always run a complete pre-presentation check, including any peripherals, such as a remote control.

The biggest drawback is reliance on electrical devices. But even there, prices of both laptop computers and projectors have dropped so low that I know several presenters who carry two of each!

Video and DVD

Pre-recorded presentation material –on video or DVD – when used well can add an invaluable air of professionalism to what would otherwise be no more than an adequate presentation. It can be used for both formal and informal meetings, product presentations, training sessions, etc. But it is *not* usually appropriate where the information involves detailed graphics, statistical information, etc.

It is also unsuitable when communicating sensitive information within a company – changes in working practices, mergers, downsizing, etc. Paradoxically, according to an Institute of Management study carried out some time ago, although 75 per cent of large British companies were using videos to communicate important changes, they also recognised that this was actually an ineffective medium for that particular kind of communication. Other studies have shown a consistently low acceptance of video amongst employees, with UK employees rating it 13th out of 16 alternative means of communication, and US employees rating it 11th out of 14.

Even with the most basic equipment a video/DVD presentation is suitable for an audience of 20–30, but this figure jumps to several hundred when using a high-powered video projector or multiple screens.

Tip:

No matter how reliable the source from which you obtain a video or DVD, even if it comes from the company learning centre, always run a videotape right through the night before you intend to use it. Nothing is worse than to find that a tape or disc is in first-class condition except for a loss of picture and/or sound right in the middle of an important statement or explanation.

If you ever try shooting your own recorded presentation, you will quickly discover why a professionally produced video costs so much to make. Pre-recorded material, on the other hand, can be hired or purchased from a number of companies at reasonable cost. This kind of presentation is particularly appropriate, and cost effective, when you want to get the same (non-sensitive) information or message to several groups at a number of separate events.

11

Designing effective visual aids

In this chapter and the next I will use the term 'graphic' to refer to DHP foils, computer displays or (photographic) slides.

Planning screen and flipchart displays

A graphic is most productive if it is a focus of attention. And a display with three or four bullet points, and three to five words per bullet, will be far more effective than a screen full of text.

The following exercise is designed to help you to make your foils as simple yet as powerful as possible:

1. Produce a graphic that includes *all* the points and details that you think should be on it.
2. Project the graphic and time yourself to see how long it takes to read *everything* on it.
3. If it takes much more than six seconds to read a particular graphic, then it needs editing!

4.Check to see how much of the text (if any) is simply a direct copy of part of your spoken material.

5. Cross out everything that isn't absolutely necessary. If you still have anything larger than key words/phrases, you haven't finished editing.

6.If more than four to five bullet points are left, either merge some of the points, or split them up over several graphics.

7. If a rehearsal leaves you changing foils almost as fast as you can speak, your bullet points are too detailed. Replan your graphics so that the bullet points are less specific.

Many people who are new to presenting seem unsure about when to use 'bullets' and when to use numbering on their graphics or slides. It isn't a subject worth getting dogmatic about, but there are two simple rules of thumb you might find useful:

- **If you are listing several elements which do not fall into a natural sequence, then use bullet points.**
- **And if there is a natural order within the elements in the display, then use numbering.**

So, if you introduce a graphic with a statement such as 'Here are some of the things you need to be aware of...', then use bullet points. And if you are using an introduction like 'Our priorities on this project, in order of importance, are...', then numbering the elements will help to reinforce the point.

Points that make a point

A much-used cliché related to training and presenting is 'Death by PowerPoint'. It is an unfortunate phrase since it implies that there is something wrong with PowerPoint itself. Personally I see the software as neutral (whichever presentation package we may choose), and the user as the deciding factor.

Which raises the question of why so many presenters still depend on a series of anonymous 'bullet points'? In a book like this, monotone 'bullets' are fine because your eye passes over them and moves on in next to no time. But in a situation where each display stays up for a couple of minutes or more it is worth replacing the standard 'blob' with something more creative:

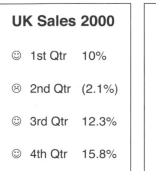

UK Sales 2000	Going for it
	The Three Ps
☺ 1st Qtr 10%	**Perseverance**
☹ 2nd Qtr (2.1%)	**Penetration**
☺ 3rd Qtr 12.3%	**Profits**
☺ 4th Qtr 15.8%	

These two layouts are actually pure text, and text can be used just like pictures. In the next example it is the visual impact which makes the display so effective (the top line reads: 'Verbal Content = 7 per cent'):

Verbal content = 7 per cent

Vocal Interest = 38 per cent

Body Language = 55 per cent

We could present the same information in more scientific manner using a pie chart:

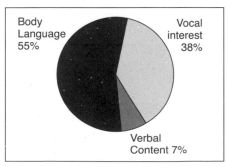

Or we can make it more eye-catching by using a touch of humour:

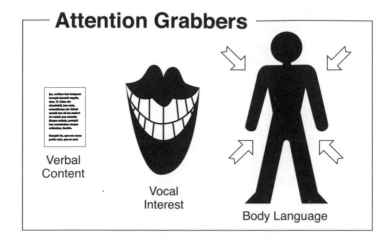

A chart (or graph) for all reasons

Charts and graphs can be an invaluable way of presenting numerical data in an easily understood format. But what is the best way of illustrating a particular piece of information?

- **KISS (Keep It Short and Simple). If the audience does not get the message in 5 to 10 seconds, they'll be watching the screen when they should be listening to you.**
- **Careful use of colours makes the information more interesting and more memorable.**
- **Use four lines per graph at most, and use a different colour for each line if the graph shows more than one line.**

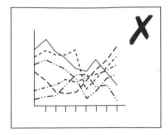
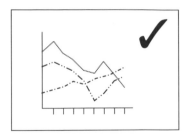

- *Line graphs* are best used to illustrate trends over a period of time, such as 'rolling' sales figures and so on. They are not suitable for illustrating precise values.
- Nor, as the diagram shows, do they work well if there are too many lines, regardless of how the lines are differentiated.
- Avoid *vertical* labels in a line graph. They are hard to read and therefore easily misread.

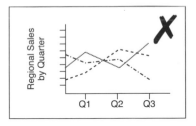
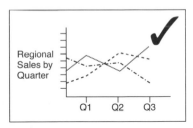

- To minimise the differences in a chart or graph make the X *axis* (the base line) as long as possible (within reason).
- To maximise the differences in a chart or graph make the vertical Y *axis* as long as possible.

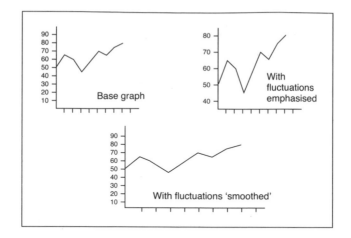

- In any kind of *bar chart*, limit each display to six or seven bars (or groups of bars) at the most.
- Use a vertical *bar chart* (with bars running from top to bottom) to compare related data at several points in time.

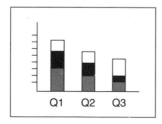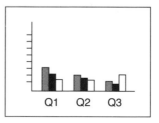

- It is sometimes quite difficult to compare the information in different bars in a '*stacked*' *bar chart*.
- So only use 'stacked' columns if the precise make-up of each column is relatively unimportant, otherwise groups of adjacent bars are more effective.

- A *horizontal bar chart* (histogram) is best suited to showing relative values for a number of related items at a given moment in time, and where the main purpose of the chart is to illustrate relative values.

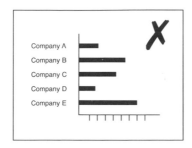 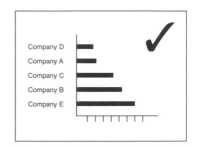

- When using a histogram *always* arrange the bars in ascending or descending order of magnitude, *not* in alphabetical order.
- A *pie chart* is often the best way of illustrating the relative values which go together to make up a single whole (for example, how a given market is currently shared out between the various manufacturers).

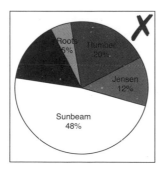 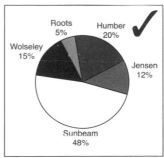

- Always put the labels for a pie chart outside the chart.
- Keep *pie charts* down to a maximum of six or seven wedges. If necessary, group some of the less important or very closely connected items under a single heading.

- Use a 'floating wedge' when you want to focus attention on that particular section of the pie (and never use more than one floating wedge per chart).

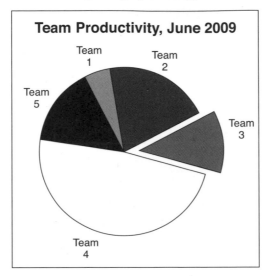

Using colour

The last 10–20 years have seen a growing interest in how the human brain works, and without going into the technical details, it seems fair to say that a presentation will be more effective if it is based on a 'whole brain' approach, rather than relying on visual aids which contain nothing but black blobs and black text, all on a white background.

The most obvious way of achieving a better result is to make sure that your visual aids really are *visual* elements – which is why this book has two whole chapters on their design, selection and use rather than the standard two or three pages. It is also worth noting that visual aids which make use of *colour* are generally more effective than black-and-white foils, slides, etc. A study by the publishing company McGraw-Hill, for example, shows that simply adding colour to an OHP foil (without making any other design changes) can improve audience retention of the data on that foil by almost 20 per cent.

The list below gives a few pointers on how your audience is likely to perceive and react to your use of colour:

- **When you use colours for text and in diagrams, aim for emphasis – not a rainbow effect. Two or three colours in a single display is usually fine; four colours can look rather excessive; and a display with five or more colours is likely to be more mind-boggling than effective.**
- **There is no reason why you shouldn't vary the colours that you use from one graphic to the next – as long as you bear the following qualification in mind:**

  If you develop some sort of colour code through your first few graphic (say black for main text, red for primary keywords and blue for secondary keywords), don't be surprised if your audience looks totally blank if you suddenly change the code to orange, green and purple for no obvious reason.
- **Always remember that *red* and *green* are the two colours most frequently involved in cases of colour blindness (which affects approximately 10 per cent of men and 0.5 per cent of women). It is a good idea to avoid these two colours when you want to emphasise a difference or a comparison.**

Tip:

When planning to use a variety of different colours – on a graphic, slide or flipchart – you can test their comparative tones (which even a person suffering from colour blindness can see) by setting out the colours on a piece of white paper and then making a black-and-white photocopy. If you cannot see a clear difference between any two 'colours' on the photocopied version, then there is a good chance that a colour-blind person may not detect any difference either.

- The colour *red* should be used, in moderation, for items which you wish to *emphasise*. It is an active, exciting colour (in its lighter, brighter shades) and will help to make the text/diagram more memorable.
- A bright, warm *yellow* is a good colour for attracting attention (when used on the right background – royal blue, dark green, maroon or sandy brown, for example). It is generally associated with positive things – sunshine, summer, warmth, etc. Unfortunately, it is also virtually invisible when used on a plain white background.
- *Dark blue* is often associated with a desire for relaxation and a degree of personal privacy. This interpretation may help to explain why medium to dark blue is best used for items which are relatively unimportant (or which you *don't* want to draw attention to).
- *Light blue*, like yellow, has positive connotations linked to clear skies, sunny days and so on. (It's no accident that *faded* denim jeans are much more popular than brand new, *dark* blue garments.) Unfortunately, *light blue* and similar colours – pale turquoise, for instance – are visually weak unless set off by complementary colours nearby.
- Although there are certain difficulties involved in using *green* and *red* together, *green* itself, in its darker shades, is a visually strong colour and is the most visible colour under poor lighting conditions.
- Generally speaking, it is a good idea to avoid the lighter shades of *green* (that is, the shades which have a large element of *yellow* in them, such as *lime-green*). These colours have very negative associations in many peoples' minds, related to sickness, etc.
- Incidentally, medium to light shades of *green* show up very badly on a white background or under a bright light.

> **Tip:**
> When selecting colours in a computer graphics program, it is useful to know what is meant by 'Hue', 'Sat' and 'Lum'.
> Hue simply means 'colour'. Changing the Hue setting will give different colours (red, yellow, green, etc) of equal brightness and intensity.
> Sat is short for 'saturation', or the intensity of the colour. Maximum saturation gives the most intense version of a colour; minimum saturation produces a shade of grey.
> Lum is an abbreviation of 'luminescence', or brightness (the presence or absence of light). For any colour, the maximum luminescence will produce white, while the minimum setting will produce black.

PowerPoint – the next generation

(In reply to reviewers who have suggested that there wasn't enough information about PowerPoint in previous editions of this book, using PowerPoint to full effect is a subject that fills whole books all on its own. In the limited space available to me, I have set out a few basic points which I hope will be of use.)

Despite the anti-*PowerPoint* rebellion in the business world over the last few years, the fact is that this product has been significantly improved at each generation, and is now far more powerful and at the same time more user friendly than it was even 10 years ago. So if slide shows for presentations are an important part of your work it's well worth getting the most up-to-date version of PowerPoint that your budget will allow – and at least one of the many expert books on how to use its facilities.

In the past, many users have been unaware of the full range of functions and facilities available to them – even in the older versions. For example, how many users know about these very basic commands which can be used when running a PowerPoint presentation with a keyboard:

- **To jump from any slide back to the first slide – press 'Home'.**
- **To jump from any slide forward to the last slide – press 'End'.**
- **To jump from any slide to any non-adjacent slide – backwards or forwards – type in the number of the required slide and press the 'Return' key.**
- **To blank the screen without ending the slide show and without moving to another slide – press 'B' to black out the screen. Press 'B' again to re-display the slide.**

You can find a list of these options by pressing F1 whilst running a slide show. (Note: The slide show need not contain more than one blank slide. Simply click on the slide show icon – bottom left of the PowerPoint window – to get the full screen display, and then press F1.)

But there's more to this than just learning how to use PowerPoint or any other presentation package well. If you want to make your presentations even more effective then you need to give special attention to the topic I mentioned earlier: the use of pictures as well as words.

Nick Oulton, in his book *Killer Presentations* (How To Books, 2005), has some very interesting ideas on how to produce visual aids which genuinely draw the audience in and get them involved with the presentation instead of being purely passive onlookers.

One of Nick's 'killer ideas' is that, even when they consist of very simple pictures, 'slides should not be self-explanatory'. Take the 'Attention Grabbers' graphic on page 100, and instead of showing the whole foil at once you might start off with this:

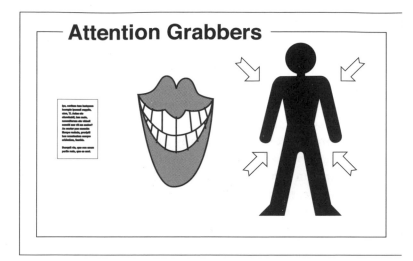

and then 'fly in' the label for each part of the graphic – 'Verbal Content', 'Vocal Interest' and 'Body Language' – one at a time, from the right, explaining what each element signifies as you build the overall picture.

By using this approach you first raise a question – what on earth does this mean? – which you then answer, thereby creating and answering a need in order to draw your audience into the presentation.

Last word on graphics

Always check what your graphics, especially your intended colour scheme, will look like in real life. All too often, inexperienced presenters assume that the effect they see on their computer will be duplicated in the presentation room. And all too often they are wrong.

Some key points to watch out for are:

- **A colour that looks good in small doses doesn't necessarily look as good when used as a main background colour. Often the exact reverse is true.**

- Print that can be read clearly on the computer screen may not be anything like as clear to the people sitting in the back row at the presentation. In practice, as we said before, anything smaller than 28pt may be unreadable from more than a metre or two (a few feet) away, and in many cases even larger fonts may be appropriate.
- Colour contrasts that are easily readable on the computer screen may be totally illegible in the presentation room. A frequent error is the use of white lettering on a medium to light background colour. In practice, white lettering, especially small white lettering, is only practical on a dark background such as navy blue or black.

Handouts

A handout, be it text, graphics or both, provides a *visual* reinforcement for the other elements of a presentation.

Apart from anything else, there is always the problem of ensuring that the members of the audience interpret your message accurately. Those with an *auditory* representational system may be completely comfortable with a purely verbal presentation. But they only make up about 25 per cent of the business population. The other 75 per cent need that back-up material or there are likely to be significant gaps in their version of what you said – which will be filled in with what they think you probably said.

Those members of the audience who tend to prefer to get their information at a high level of *chunking* ('give me the facts but spare me the details') may find it relatively difficult to stay attentive if your presentation follows the usual progression from individual facts up to overall picture. An interesting and imaginative handout will help to focus their attention.

In short, a handout helps to ensure that your audience get the message, the whole message and nothing but the message.

But when should you hand out the handouts: before, during or after the presentation?

- If you distribute the handout(s) *before* the presentation (by leaving a copy on each seat, or by handing it to people as they come in) you really have no control over what people do with it.
- If you distribute handouts at the start of each *subsection* of an event, some people may read ahead but at least they will be limited to material that is to be covered within the current session.
- If you don't make the handout(s) available until *after* the event (by having someone pass them out as people leave, perhaps) you can be sure that no one will read ahead.

On the other hand:

- People don't usually get diverted by the handout(s) unless they are bored with the presentation.
- If the presentation is mainly a detailed explanation of the foils in the handout, people will appreciate being able to make notes directly alongside the relevant illustrations.
- It is a presenter's job to produce an interesting and informative presentation – not to police the audience.

The key factor that decides when to circulate a handout is purely utilitarian: when should it be distributed to achieve the greatest benefit for the maximum number of people?

Colour in handouts

If you ever think of producing handouts on coloured paper, you may be interested to know, in theory at least, that the most readable colour combination is black print on a *canary yellow* background. Such a document would be even more stimulating (with negligible loss of visibility) if an occasional pastel pink/ blue/green page were included amongst the yellow.

Having said that, it is generally more effective to use coloured pages sparingly in a handout as this may be seen by many business people as frivolous in the context of a formal business presentation or meeting. On a training course, however, using different coloured paper can be a useful way to make the handouts for different sections of the event instantly identifiable.

Using black and white or coloured illustrations on the other hand, can be a significant cost factor. Printing in colour should not be ruinous if done in-house, but can be markedly more expensive than black and white if it is outsourced. Photocopying in colour is not a reasonable option unless you have very few illustrations, or money is no object.

12

Setting the scene

Anyone for tennis?

When it comes to setting up your display facilities – flipchart, OHP or projector, etc – there are two basic options. The first alternative – the 'head on' position – places the screen directly facing the audience. The second option has the screen to one side and at an angle to the audience.

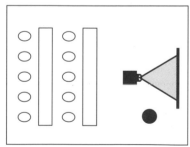 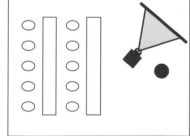

If the screen is placed at an angle to the audience they must look at you, or the screen, but not both. If the screen is placed centre stage they can see the display and you at the same time. Assuming that you have designed your foils or slides correctly, they should be simple enough to focus the viewers' attention on what you are saying, thereby reinforcing it.

Incidentally, you may not have a choice about where the screen is positioned. Many presentation facilities have the screen in a fixed location (usually in the 'head on' position). If you are likely to be doing a number of presentations, working at several different sites, it is worth practising with both set-ups so that you feel comfortable in either setting.

Please be seated

Once you have located your screen, you need to seat your audience. A minor point of little interest? Not so! Seating arrangements can have a profound effect on the way that members of the audience respond to both the presenter and the presentation.

If it is up to you to arrange the seating at a presentation, you need to take account of two main factors:

- **audience size;**
- **degree of interaction required between members of the audience and between the audience and the presenter.**

The intimate brainstorm

For small groups, and situations where you want the atmosphere to be reasonably open and a certain degree of discussion is expected, the appropriate seating arrangement will be the *Round table* or the *Open circle*:

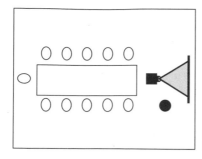
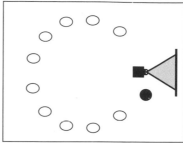

Round table layout   **Open circle layout**

The Round table layout is appropriate if the audience will need a flat surface for drinks, to write notes, and so on. Where the main activity is to be a discussion, and will last for an hour or two at most, the Open circle seating plan may be more effective in allowing communication between the participants.

> **Note:** These seating plans are unsuitable for groups of more than 20–24 people, and work best with groups of 12–15 people.

Divided to conquer

Two commonly used seating layouts for medium-sized groups (say 20–30 people) are the *Open square* and the *Block*. They are easily adapted to fit wide rooms or narrow rooms and a variety of audience sizes with very little trouble:

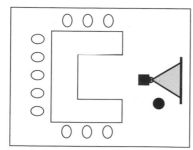
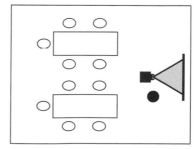

Open square layout   **Block layout**

These set-ups can be used for informal or formal presentations, as well as training sessions and any type of group which involves a certain degree of discussion, but which does not require the relative intimacy of the Round table or the Open circle.

The main weakness of the Open square is that it reinforces the position of the presenter as the focus of attention, thus doing very little to encourage any team feeling.

For situations where a sense of team membership is an integral part of the event, you may prefer to use the Block seating plan. This seating arrangement creates individual groupings within the audience as a whole, and thereby encourages a team feeling and a greater willingness to interact as a group rather than just as individuals.

The downside of using seating order is the fact that the people seated along the inside edge of each block need to turn sideways-on to the table in order to see the screen or flipchart. This could be a hinderance is required to do a great deal of note-taking during the presentation, and in such cases the Open square plan would be preferable.

Come one, come all

For larger audiences (30 and over), there are three basic seating plans: the *Conference*, the *Restaurant* and the *Theatre*.

The main factors affecting your choice between these three plans are:

- **How long is the event?**
- **Are the members of the audience required to take notes, or merely sit, look and listen?**
- **How much room is available in relation to the size of the audience?**

The Conference layout allows a medium to high level of interaction between audience and presenter, and is indicated where:

- the event will last at least one full day;
- the audience will need to take notes;
- only low to medium interaction is required between members of the audience;
- finding a large enough room to run the presentation with chairs and tables will not be a problem.

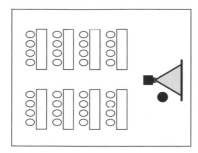

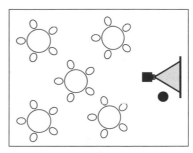

| Conference layout | Restaurant layout |

The Restaurant style of seating is much favoured by some of the top business presenters, allowing a high level of interaction between the presenter and their audience (especially if the presenter uses the seating area as part of their own working space). It is often the only seating option available if the presentation is being run in an hotel which does not have specialised conference facilities.

It is also an arrangement which favours high interaction between members of the audience, if required, and can serve to enhance team identity (at the table-by-table level). Unfortunately, however, this same group identification can mean trouble for a presenter who is not used to working in this kind of situation and group activities can easily spill over into the presentation sessions.

Generally speaking, this layout is really only indicated where:

- the event will *not* last for more than one full day;
- the audience will need to do very little note-taking;
- the presenter has well-developed 'crowd control' abilities.

A further feature of this type of layout is the fact that it is inevitable that at least one or two people at each table (depending on the size of the tables) will need to spend most of their time facing towards the presentation area and away from the table. Many people find this arrangement somewhat unsettling and for that reason alone it is best avoided if possible. One way round this problem is to have chairs round only the back half of the table – possibly an unacceptable waste of space where large numbers of people must be accommodated.

The last option – the Theatre seating plan – is most suitable where:

- **the event will last for no more than one full day;**
- **the audience will not need to take notes;**
- **interaction between the audience and the presenter is not a key feature of the event;**
- **no room can be found which is large enough to accommodate a presentation with both chairs and tables.**

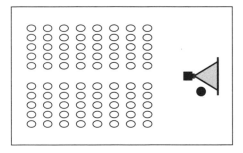

Theatre seating plan

This is another style of seating much favoured in hotel-based presentations. Unfortunately, hotel chairs are seldom of a sort designed for comfortable sitting over a prolonged period and this fact should be allowed for by providing correspondingly frequent comfort breaks.

If you want it done properly

One last word of warning before we leave the subject of seating arrangements. Do remember that hotel staff, even at line management level, are frequently overworked and not particularly well trained, especially as far as conferences, etc are concerned. Moreover many staff may be from other countries and have a less-than-perfect grasp of the English language. So like the proverbial Boy Scout – Be Prepared.

- *Never* assume that hotel staff will automatically know how to prepare a room for a presentation.
- *Always* provide clear instructions in advance, preferably including a diagram of the required layout, and check that they have been received by the relevant person.
- *Always* check the room layout for yourself on the day of the event *in plenty of time for it to be changed, if necessary.*

So many switches – so few hands

Only experience will teach you all the precautions that you need to take when doing a presentation away from home. Listed below are some of the most important pointers to setting up an effective presentation:

- When using electrical equipment always start by checking the location of the power outlets. Provide your own 'gang plug' and an extension lead to avoid difficulties caused by badly placed power outlets.
- Is everything set up correctly? Have you checked *every* piece of electrical equipment?
- If you're using any kind of projector, check that the screen and projector are correctly angled in relation to each other (the front of the projector and the screen should be parallel). If the projected image is larger on

one side of the screen then pull that side of the screen forwards (towards the projector) until both sides of the image are equal.

- When using an OHP, make sure that you have room to stack used and unused foils in separate, easy-to-reach piles. Experiment to find an arrangement that feels comfortable, bearing in mind the need to stay clear of the screen area when changing foils.
- When using a computer-linked projector, make sure that you have some kind of blocks you can use to adjust the angle of the projector. In some situations the 'screw out' leg may be way too short to get the angle right.
- Check the heating/air conditioning controls. How accurate are they? Can they be easily reset? (In older buildings it may be difficult to control the heating on a room-by-room basis.)

  Keep the room slightly cool, even when full of people, in order to keep the members of the audience from getting so comfortable that they start to doze off.

- If the room/hall is large enough to require a sound system, is the microphone set at the right height (or are you going to be using a wireless microphone)? In either case, make sure that you do a proper sound check *before* the event.

  Few things are more unnerving than to start speaking and be interrupted by electronic feedback – the audible equivalent of sticking a knitting needle in one ear and out of the other. Feedback occurs when the output from one device (usually one of the speakers) is being picked up by the microphone, then sent back to the speaker, which feeds it to the microphone, and so on. (By the way, the signal from the speaker may not be loud enough to cause feedback until someone speaks into the microphone, so always do the sound check even if everything seems OK.)

- If someone else is turning lights on and off for you during your presentation, make sure that the two of you run a last-minute rehearsal. If necessary, run several rehearsals until you are both sure that you understand what needs to be done.

- If the lighting causes intrusive reflections, can you turn some lights off? If several lights are controlled by a single switch and you don't want to turn them all off, can you remove some of the bulbs to get the required result?
- Check the audience area. Are there any broken seats? Get rid of them. Are there any soiled table covers? Have them replaced. If you are providing notepads, pens, handouts, soft drinks or water, and so on, is everything correctly set out?
- Check your own area. Do you know what adjustments you will need to make (if any) after the previous speaker has finished?
- Do you have a carafe of water and a glass on hand (see Chapter 14)?
- If a lectern is provided, is it the right height? Does the light work (if any)?
- Use clearly visible tape to hold down, and mark, any electric cables that could trip someone up.

The little things that count

Finally, having ensured that the presentation room is ready for business, there are just a few last little touches that will help to make your audience feel comfortable during the event:

- Where will tea and coffee be served *before* the presentation begins?
  Having the smell of good quality coffee wafting around is a well-known way of making a home more attractive to potential buyers. If you have the space, why not make the presentation room seem more welcoming by

serving the first tea and coffee of the day at the back of the presentation room itself.

- Make sure that the staff responsible for clearing the crockery away won't interrupt the presentation. If possible, have refreshments served in another room.
- Now that smoking, and especially passive smoking, is a major social issue, you will need to designate specific smoking and non-smoking areas.
- Where appropriate, provide each delegate with a map of the venue and/or written instructions giving the routes between the presentation room and the main exit, the nearest fire exit (and assembly point), and the toilet facilities.
- Check the number of seats against the number of delegates. (If you aren't sure exactly how many seats will be needed, put out as many seats as you think you will need, and have some spare chairs stacked away in a corner.)
- If you're working with fixed seating, and there are clearly more seats than delegates, rope off the back row(s) of the audience area, and put out some 'RESERVED' notices.

And then the lights went out

What would you do if your entire presentation revolves around some kind of electrical equipment and at the very last moment it all breaks down? Worse still, what are you going to do if something goes wrong with the equipment during your presentation?

- You can panic.
- You can fall back on Plan B.

Any presenter who works with electrical devices should always have a Plan B. With a good Plan B, you can carry on regardless (using a different medium), instead of grinding to a humiliating halt as you hear that delicate 'pop' of exploding equipment.

Your personal Plan B will depend on which visual aids you are using, but here is one of the most common back-up systems. No matter whether you're using an OHP or projector, a video or a film, be sure to duplicate all your main displays on a flipchart (flipcharts never blow a fuse or a bulb). This means extra work, of course, but if you ever have to fall back on Plan B it will save your presentation and your face.

And if nothing goes wrong? Then at least you will have had the comfort and reassurance of knowing that you were prepared for any eventuality.

13

Question and answer sessions

Why?

Here are just three of the many good reasons why you might want to accept questions from your audience:

- **To create positive interaction between the members of the audience and yourself.**
- **By accepting audience questions during a presentation any misunderstandings can be cleared up immediately.**
- **The questions that you get from the audience will give you a clearer idea of their level of understanding and areas of special interest, allowing you to fine-tune your performance 'on the spot'.**

When?

Your options on taking questions are basically limited to:

- **during the presentation;**

- after you've finished the presentation;
- any time.

We've already seen some advantages of the 'any time' approach, but it also has, as you might expect, its disadvantages:

- **You may get sidetracked by questions that are not strictly relevant.**
- **Questioners frequently ask about things that are of special concern to them as individuals, but which may not be of much interest to anyone else.**
- **It is very easy to lose track of time whilst answering questions so you end up having to rush through the last part of the presentation, in order to end on time.**
- **In a 'worst case' scenario the questions could take up so much time that you cannot complete the presentation.**
- **An unexpected or awkward question may disrupt the flow of the presentation and leave you looking ill-informed and unprofessional.**

Taking control of audience questions

One simple and very effective way of allowing questions whilst still keeping the presentation on track goes like this:

> I'll take any questions that call for clarification at any time during the presentation, but any questions which require *additional information*, or which relate to anything *not* directly covered in the presentation will be dealt with at the end of the session.

This approach assures the audience that you will cover all questions before the event is over, and also gives you the option of answering a question or putting it on hold as you see fit.

The three basic secrets of handling questions

Secret no. 1

It is a natural reaction to start working out the answer to a question whilst the questioner is still speaking. Unfortunately, it is impossible to give your full attention to two separate lines of thought at the same time.

So, while a questioner is speaking, *listen*. Cut a long-winded question short, by all means, but only start thinking about the answer *when the question is complete*.

Secret no. 2

A common pitfall, when taking questions, occurs when only the presenter, the questioner and the first few rows of the audience know what question the presenter is answering. Fortunately there is a remarkably simple solution. Except in one special case (which will be covered in a later section) whenever you receive a question:

- *Rephrase* the question and then *repeat it* to the whole audience *before* you answer it;
- Then address your answer to the *whole* audience.

This action has three distinct advantages:

- If the questioner does not correct your rephrased version of the question, you can be reasonably sure that you have both heard the question correctly *and* understood it.
- Everyone in the audience knows what is going on.
- You can think about five times faster than you can speak, so by repeating the question you give yourself valuable extra time in which to think about your answer.

Secret no. 3

Avoid the trap of allowing yourself to be monopolised by just a handful of questioners.

Once you have accepted and repeated a question, aim to regulate your eye contact in the ratio of 20–25 per cent to the questioner, 75–80 per cent to the rest of the audience.

Looking at someone as you finish speaking is an implied cue for a reply. Only look at the questioner as you finish your answer *if you actually want the dialogue to continue*. Then you might also reinforce the message by asking something like: 'Does that answer your question?'

To avoid a follow-on question, simply direct your gaze to some other part of the room as you finish speaking, and indicate that you are ready to take a *new* question.

What to do when you don't know the answer

Be honest. Say 'I don't know' or, better still, 'I don't know, but I will find out'.

An even better response would be: 'I don't know, but I will find out by the end of the lunch break/tomorrow morning/etc.' And then make sure that you do.

An excuse is a loaded gun

Making excuses – for being late, for losing your place, for not knowing an answer or any other slip-up – is a dangerous move. The excuse may be entirely true, but in the long run it solves nothing and excuses always tend to sound extremely feeble, even when they are true.

The football fan

From time to time you may come across a 'football fan' demanding an 'instant replay'. In other words, someone who asks a question you are quite confident was answered in full during your presentation, or is effectively the same as a question that has already been asked and answered.

You may be tempted to respond with a statement such as: 'I believe I've already answered that', which might sound polite on the surface, but is actually a slap in the face to the questioner as it implies that they were too stupid or inattentive to catch the explanation first time round.

Alternatively you might be inclined to answer with something like, 'I beg your pardon; I obviously didn't make myself clear', but this can sound patronising, as though the questioner may have heard the previous explanation but hadn't the brains to understand it.

The better response is to ignore the fact that you've covered the material before and repeat the question and answer it – but this time only answer the specific point the questioner has asked about, thus keeping your answer brief. And who knows, as you restate the information the questioner may catch on to the fact that you've already covered that material.

Dr Heckle

Dr Heckle 'questioners' don't really want to ask a question so much as make a provocative or disruptive statement. This is one time when you definitely *should not* repeat what has been put to you, unless the question/statement reflects to your benefit. Three easy actions will stop this kind of heckling:

- **Ask the 'questioner' to identify themself. This breaks the audience's concentration, gives you extra time to prepare an answer, and starts to defuse the troublesome statement.**

- Review the statement, looking for the underlying motive.
- Use your analysis of the statement to rephrase it as a question, so that the content is no longer antagonistic to your own position.

For example, the 'statement':

> I can't see how you expect to increase the sales of Fanshaw's patent widgets when 50 per cent of our output is returned within six months!

seems likely to be a not very veiled criticism of the way that Fanshaw's Patent Widgets are being manufactured. Which might be a subject worth discussing – at some other time.

It would make sense, then, to reword the question in a less confrontational manner, as another question:

> OK, Joan has made a very good point here – how can we improve our production standards so as to increase our sales?
>
> I think we should start by looking at the factors which have a direct influence on those standards.

You don't have to distort a statement in order to turn it into a question, and if someone makes a statement so loaded that you'd rather not deal with it at all, simply defer it thus:

> That's not really something I can give a straight 'yes' or 'no' answer to, but I'll be happy to discuss it with you in more detail when we break for coffee/lunch/tea.

Mr Jibe

A 'Mr Jibe' differs from a Dr Heckle by appearing to be siding with and assisting the presenter. Mr Jibe's questions usually start with a phrase such as: 'Isn't it true that...?'

The problem lies in the ambiguity of this opening phrase. The question may be an attempt to show off, or it may be a deliberate attempt to trap you into a mistake. It might even be a genuine question! In order to respond effectively to a 'Mr Jibe', whatever their motive, make sure that you adhere to the guidelines we've already discussed:

1. Wait until the question/statement is complete.
2. Reframe what has been said, using a lead-in phrase such as: 'If I've understood you correctly, you're saying [reframed statement]. Have I got that right?'
3. Be especially careful that you only answer Mr Jibe if you are sure of your facts. Otherwise, simply say something like, 'Well that's an interesting idea. I'll have to look into it when we take a break.'

No matter how confident Mr Jibe may sound, and no matter how plausible his comments, *never* assume that he knows what he is talking about.

Beware the 'early bird'

An 'early bird' is a character who simply cannot wait to get at the 'worm' – the part of the presentation that they are particularly interested in. If the worm doesn't appear in what they consider to be a reasonable time, then they just has to get in there to try to rootle it out with a probing question.

The best way to deal with an early bird is to give them recognition and cut the question short all in one go, thus:

> I do plan to cover that topic a little later on. Let me jot your question down so that I don't forget to answer it when we get to the appropriate point.

This response reassures the questioner that their enquiry has been taken seriously and will be addressed, but leaves no room for further discussion.

Bones of contention

Some time or other you are bound to run into a 'hidden absolute' – a 'question' that starts with a phrase like:

Everyone knows that...
It's quite obvious that...

To take the sting out of this kind of question: *act dumb and ask for validation*. There is, of course, a right and a wrong way to do this, depending on whether you concentrate on the question or on the questioner. For example, let's suppose that Chris, a member of the audience, decides to question a course of action proposed by the presenter:

Chris: 'It must be obvious to everyone here that [this course of action] is bound to fail.'
Presenter: 'Hands up anyone who agrees with Chris.'

In practice Chris may realise, as soon as he makes the comment, that it can, at most, only apply to everyone *except* the presenter, but the fact is that he said 'everyone'. And that's why a calm response is bound to win out. An absolute can only be true if it is *absolutely true*. Yet we already know that the presenter at least believes that the action will succeed, so the hidden absolute cannot be true.

Unfortunately this first reaction from the presenter has three important weaknesses:

1. The vote has now become a popularity contest.
2. Did everyone hear what Chris said?
3. The presenter has missed a golden opportunity to provide an alternative point of view.

A far better response might go like this:

It has been suggested that the proposed action may not be completely successful. As the proposer of this action I can't agree with that, but what do other people think?

Would the people who don't agree with the proposal like to raise their hands.

This second response:

1. Turns the original statement into a suggestion.
2. Demonstrates that the hidden absolute is incorrect, but without being confrontational.
3. Turns the vote into a 'sounding out' exercise, thereby removing the emotional charge.
4. Proposes the vote in negative terms. Since most people dislike agreeing to a negative proposition, this will minimise the support for the original statement.

Alternatively, the presenter could have asked a question such as: 'I wonder what makes you think that?' (An abrupt 'Why do you say that?' is definitely *not* the right way to tackle this kind of situation.)

Don't be afraid to hand the floor over to the speaker for a short while. When you think they've said enough simply thank them politely for their opinion and insist that time constraints mean that you must move on to the next question.

The Phantom

The Phantom questioner is more interested in hypothetical questions and answers than in practicalities. Thus their questions tend to start with phrases like: 'What if...', 'If we assume...' and 'Just suppose...', etc.

The reason why a Phantom may seem dangerous lies in the fear that, if you don't respond to their hypothetical scenario, then you may look as though you don't have the ability to plan ahead. Against this you have to consider what will happen if the Phantom questioner uses your initial answer as an excuse to indulge in further speculation. In next to no time you could find yourself adrift in a sea of pure conjecture.

In practice, whilst it would be foolhardy to take action without making some kind of contingency planning, there is always a limit to how useful it is to set out *detailed* 'safety nets' before you've even started to put a policy into effect. It may also be taken as a sign of lack of confidence on your part if you acknowledge that you are already thinking about what to do if your plans don't work out.

One way to handle a Phantom is to gently emphasise the speculative nature of their question. For example:

> As I understand your question, you are asking me to guess what might happen if this development did not go according to plan.
>
> Firstly, let me assure you that I have every confidence that the development will be successful.
>
> Secondly, I don't think it would be useful to give you an answer which would be purely hypothetical and might bear little or no relation to whatever action we actually decide to take in the future.

Happy Wanderers

At some time or other you may come across a 'Happy Wanderer', someone who starts out ostensibly asking a question but quickly gets lost in a convoluted speech which may or may not be related to the question they first thought of.

The way you handle a Wanderer depends on what you think is really going on:

- **If you think the Wanderer has a genuine, constructive point to make then you might say something like:**

Pardon me for interrupting – you have obviously given this some careful thought. Unfortunately we only have a limited time for questions and I must ask you to summarise the point you wish to make so that other people have a chance to speak.

- **On the other hand, if you think the Wanderer has 'lost the plot' and has no useful point to make, or that they are being deliberately obstructive, you might use an approach such as:**

I must interrupt you there. I appreciate that you are concerned about this matter, but I'm not clear what question you wish to ask. Since we only have a limited time I must ask you to state your question very briefly so that we can move on.

- **And with any Happy Wanderer, regardless of what you think their motives might be, an alternative response would be to interrupt them with a statement such as:**

Thank you for your thoughts. Unfortunately we only have a limited time for questions so I'm going to have to move on. However, I'll be happy to discuss this with you in more detail when we come to the break.

   Then turn to another area of the audience, where someone else looked like they wanted to speak, and say:

Yes? I think I saw a hand up over here...?

- **If the person still goes on speaking then you will need to deal with the situation as you would for a heckler.**

The good, the bad and the ugly

With adequate preparation, dealing with genuine questions should not be a problem. Even the odd 'difficult customer' can be handled using the following procedure:

Step 1 – relax

Your natural reaction to a loud, contentious or rude 'question' from the audience may well be to tense up, with throat dry and heart beating faster as extra adrenalin is pumped around your bloodstream. To counter these reactions, allow yourself to mentally withdraw for a moment and say to yourself: 'I am thinking about the fact that I am experiencing an emotional reaction.'

The process of thinking rationally about your feelings will enable you to view the situation more calmly, and to deal with it appropriately.

Step 2 – be firm and polite

No matter how bad things look, be firm and polite. An audience will only support a presenter against a heckler as long as the presenter is *perceived* to be in control of themselves.

Step 3 – check the audience's body language

This will give you some important clues about what to do next:

- If people are exchanging looks and settling back as though they know what's coming next, you are probably dealing with a regular heckler whose actions are seen by their colleagues as a form of entertainment. See Step 4, Option 1.
- If people are paying more attention to the heckler than to you then they are probably in agreement with what is being said. See Step 4, Option 2.
- If people look irritated and are watching you rather than the heckler, then they probably regard the heckler's comments as an unwelcome intrusion. In this case, they

will tend to be on your side rather than the heckler's, and they will expect you to resolve the situation as soon as possible. See Step 4, Option 1.
- When all else fails, see Step 4, Option 3.

Step 4 – Option 1

If you think that a heckler is simply sounding off, ask them what answer *they* would give. Remain calm and courteous until the heckler runs out of steam, or the other members of the audience begin to look bored, then bring the incident to a close with a polite but firm acknowledgement such as:

> Well, you clearly have very strong views on this matter, but I think we've gone as far as we can on this subject and I'm afraid I'm going to have to move on…

Maintain eye contact with the heckler for the first part of your response, but then make an obvious point of looking away – in search of further questions or comments – as you finish.

Step 4 – Option 2

When a questioner appears to have considerable support from other members of the audience, you will need to make a tactical decision as to the consequences of continuing the discussion.

Above all, be honest. The audience may not like your answer if it turns out that you cannot give the answer they want, but most people *can* see when they're being told the truth. If you stand your ground in a reasonable manner, it is more than likely that you will carry the day.

Step 4 – Option 3

If nothing else works, you may have to cut a heckler short. Make it clear that you feel that you have done all you can to satisfy the heckler's demands and can do no more.

If you have indeed played fair with the heckler, the other members of the audience will probably help to settle the matter for you by a show of mass disapproval.

In the seats of power

So far we've dealt with situations where the presenter is fielding questions single-handedly, either during or immediately after the presentation. From time to time, however, you may find that you are called upon to answer questions as a member of a panel. At first glance this may seem to be a situation where the chairman, as mediator between the audience and the members of the panel, will have a high degree of control. To an outsider, it might seem that members of the panel will simply come in with their individual contributions as and when they are called upon to do so. In reality things are a little more complicated than that, and the activities of each panel member tends to reflect their physical location in relation to the chairman.

In some cases, the seating arrangements may be made in advance so that panel members have no say as to where they will sit. On other occasions it may be a question of taking your seat in order of entry on to the platform, or you may simply be allowed to sit wherever you chose. Even when the seating is pre-arranged, it may be possible to get the chairman's agreement to a slight re-arrangement, especially if no one else understands the significance of the various seating positions.

Many panel sessions have all of the members of the panel, plus the chairman, sitting in a straight line, as shown in this next illustration.

The numbers in the circles on each side of the chairman indicate the relative influence of the person in that position (where the greater the number, the greater the influence). The only two seats of power on a straight line arrangement are

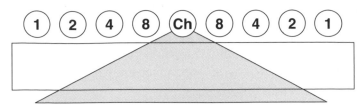

Chairman's Lines of Sight

the seats immediately next to the chairman. The two people in seats numbered 8 not only have the ability to pass notes to the chairman, or even speak directly to them – they can also intercept messages passed to the chairman by other panel members, should they wish to do so. The chairman's natural sight lines to the audience do not take in any of the panel members; the chairman must deliberately look to their left or right in order to be aware of any hand signals from members of the panel.

Where the panel is arranged in an open square (see next diagram), two further panel members are brought into the equation, because they intercept the sightlines between the chairman and the audience. This allows the people in the seats numbered 5 to catch the chairman's attention, even though they cannot communicate directly.

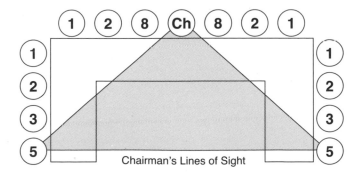

Chairman's Lines of Sight

It follows from these two diagrams, that it is relatively easy (assuming that you have the choice of deciding where to sit) to decide whether to maximise or minimise your chance of taking an active part in the proceedings.

Some chairmen know how to ensure that everyone on the panel gets a fair crack of the whip. It may also turn out that your presentation, or at least your specialised knowledge, will attract a fair number of questions.

In practice, however, chairmen are invariably selected on the basis of availability rather than skill, and it is far more likely that the part you play in the panel discussion will be dictated by the 'Chairman's Line of Sight' rules:

1. Your ability to control your part in a panel discussion is directly related to your ability to catch the chairman's attention, because...
2. The harder it is for the chairman to see you, the less likely it is that they will aim any questions in your direction.

14

Personal presentation

Here I stand

It is truly amazing how easy it is to become self-conscious about your body when you give your first few presentations. How should you stand or move, for example?

- **No matter what you may have read or heard, moving around is no better, and no worse, than standing still.**
- **When standing still, aim to have your feet about shoulder width apart and keep your body square on to the audience and with your toes pointing slightly outwards. This stance is comfortable to maintain and indicates to the audience that you are relaxed and confident.**
- **Make sure that you are clearly visible to your audience, especially when you are saying something important. If you stand in front of a bright light, such as a well-lit window, your audience won't see much more than a black shape (which will literally be perceived as a negative image).**

Here are some important 'posture pointers':

- **Settling in one spot, leaning to one side.**
  Hidden message: **'I'm bored and I'd rather be somewhere else.'**
  Solution: **When standing still, keep your weight evenly balanced and your hips level.**
- **Leaning over the top of the lectern.**
  Hidden message: **'I'm too tired to stand up straight – or I just can't be bothered to do so.'**
  Solution: **When using a lectern, avoid temptation by standing to one side rather than directly behind it.**
- **Sitting on the table provided for your notes, the OHP, etc.**
  Hidden message: **'I don't have to make an effort here, because I'm more important than you.'**
  Solution: **No matter how relaxed you feel, stay standing!**

In short, there is no ideal stance. Within reason, do whatever feels right for *you*. It is far more important that your verbal content, vocal style and body language should be congruent (all giving the same message) than whether you walk 3 metres or 3 kilometres while delivering your presentation.

You've got to hand it to them

The best way to use your hands during a presentation is to act as though you were in a normal conversation. If you usually wave your hands around in an animated fashion do the same thing (within reason) in a presentation. And if you don't usually make much use of your hands when you're talking, that's fine, too. In short, if it doesn't feel comfortable don't do it – and don't worry about it, either. The members of your audience have no idea what to expect from you, and what they never see they won't miss.

> ## Tip:
> If it feels natural to use your hands when talking, make sure that your gestures during a presentation are appropriate for the size of your audience. Thus the more people you are talking to, the bigger your hand and arm movements will need to be.

It may help you to decide what to do with your hands if you rehearse in front of the mirror or a close friend, to see what impression you will create.

Here are some poses you might want to avoid:

- **The 'stand at ease' stance – feet firmly planted and hands clasped behind your back. This looks stiff and overly formal. It is an 'authoritarian' stance, and will make it much harder to establish a rapport with your audience.**
- **Having your hands in your pockets looks unduly casual, or even sloppy. Having said that, if you find that your hands have wandered into your pockets:**
  - **Remove your hand(s) from your pocket(s) in a leisurely manner at a suitable moment (to point at something in a visual display for instance.**
  - **And for the men, if your hands find their way into your trouser pockets then above all, keep them still. If you fiddle with something in your pocket, no matter how innocent you may be, at least half of your audience will interpret your actions in the worst possible way!**
- **Clasping your hands in front of you in the 'fig leaf' position looks rigid and uncomfortable and in English-speaking countries is generally recognised as a *defensive* posture, particularly for men. This stance will tend to**

set you apart from your audience and will lower your esteem in their eyes. It won't do much for your own self-confidence either.

- Standing with your hands on your hips can look arrogant, affected or just plain silly, depending on your general physique. This was a favourite pose of the late Benito Mussolini, and look what happened to him.
- Folding your arms over your stomach or chest can appear domineering in a large person, and is otherwise recognised as a defensive or divisive posture.
- Rubbing your hands together in a 'washing' motion looks creepy, fussy and possibly dishonest.

Just one look

We covered the key elements of making eye contact with your audience in Chapter 4, and there are only a couple of brief comments I want to add here:

- As far as timing is concerned, you should look at any single person for no more than three or four seconds (about the time it takes to say 'One banana, two banana, three banana, four banana'). Shift your focus of attention frequently and preferably randomly (it is quite distracting to see an inexperienced presenter sweeping their gaze back and forth like some kind of human searchlight).
- In general terms, then, you will want to maintain eye contact with your audience as a whole, though there are times when it can actually be beneficial if you deliberately *break* eye contact:
  - If you ask your audience to think something through for a few moments you lead the way by breaking eye contact and then mime being thoughtful until you are ready to continue.

- If you want people to look at the screen or flipchart, whether or not you are writing on the flipchart or putting up a new graphic, stop speaking and turn towards the display yourself. Don't turn back or start speaking again until you think people have had sufficient time to take in what you want them to look at.

To sum up, the overall image that you need to project for the best effect is one of relaxed control. This impression is most easily produced if it reflects what you really feel – when you know that you've done everything you can to ensure that the presentation goes well.

Four keys to success

If this book were distilled into four key points they would be:

- Know your audience
  Who do you really need to talk to? What do you want them to hear? How do you want them to react? What will motivate them to respond in the desired manner?
- Keep it simple
  Language is an extremely inadequate medium for expressing any but the most simple ideas. So KISS (Keep It Short and Simple), and always talk to your audience as they are, not as you would like them to be.
- Keep to the point
  Don't underestimate your audience – but don't overestimate them, either. Be realistic. You only have a limited timeframe in which to tell your audience what they need to know, not everything that you know.
- Have confidence in yourself and in your message
  The audience will usually be on your side, at least at the start of the presentation. If you look confident and

sound confident (but not arrogant) it is very probable
that you will keep them on your side, even if you do
make the odd mistake. You are far more likely to lose
that goodwill by being pompous or timid than by
fluffing your lines, putting up the wrong graphic, or by
running into an odd heckler.

Style of speaking

Given that we develop our way of speaking over many years, can
we really hope to develop a whole new vocal style?

Why not? All it takes is that you should *want* to improve
your verbal skills. And the word *improve* really is crucial in this
respect. Think of this as a progressive process, as an extension of
your abilities.

Practise in front of a mirror and by talking into a tape
recorder or a video camera. It doesn't really matter *what* you say
at this point so much as *how* you say it. Find ways to make your
voice more interesting, more expressive and more authoritative.
As the ultimate test, read a column from your local telephone
directory so that it sounds exciting, amusing or persuasive. You'll
be amazed at how quickly you can begin to develop your vocal
skills.

Taking care of your voice

The *Big Ben* exercise (also known as the *King Kong* routine) is an
easy yet effective way of deepening your voice and enhancing
its flexibility. Make yourself comfortable, taking care that you
are not constricting your chest or diaphragm in any way. Now,
starting in your normal tone of voice, work your way down the
scale singing 'ding, dong, bing, bong'. Keep going until you reach
the lowest note that you can manage without straining your

vocal cords. Then work your way up the scale until you reach the highest note that you can manage without strain. Finally, work your way back down the scale until you reach your normal tone of voice.

Repeat this exercise four or five times each session, one or two sessions per day, and you'll be amazed at the results. Your normal speaking voice will deepen; the range of notes that you can cover (without stress) will widen; and your voice will become more flexible, more varied and, above all, more interesting.

As well as developing an interesting and flexible speaking voice, remember to exercise it, take care of it, and during the colder months, take care that your throat is well protected when you go outside. Always take the appropriate kind of medication if you detect any sign of soreness or irritation.

Rehearsals

Your rehearsal(s) for a presentation should be part of the process of preparing your script.

Once you have drafted the outline of your script, put it on audio tape (videotape is even better) then run it through with the following thoughts in mind:

- **Does your presentation follow a clear sequence of ideas?**
- **Have you aimed the material at the right level?**
- **Have you included material that isn't strictly relevant?**
- **Are you trying to cover too much information?**
- **How and where can you use visual aids to clarify and enhance the basic presentation?**
- **Are you presenting your material in an appropriate manner?**

Armed with the answers to these questions, and any others which seem important to you, work your first draft into something more precise.

Tip:
Whilst rehearsing, make sure you learn the first two minutes of your presentation (about 250–300 words) by heart.

By the way, rehearsals are especially important when a presentation is to be a team project. Even if all the members of the team are experienced presenters, at least one team rehearsal is necessary:

- **To make sure that 'handing on the baton' goes smoothly at each change of presenter.**
- **To check the timing of each section of the presentation.**
- **To check the material – it is not unknown (when rehearsals don't take place) for one member of the team to stray beyond the topic assigned to them and thus pre-empt the comments planned by a later speaker.**
- **To ensure that the presentation has the appearance of a well-coordinated production. Many people attending a team presentation, especially potential customers, will place quite a lot of importance on how well the presenters work together *as a team*. Rightly or wrongly, members of the audience may assume that the ability of the team members to work together – or not – is an indication of how well their company works in general.**

Can you hear me at the back?

When you think that you've developed a script that does what you want it to do, have another recorded rehearsal, asking yourself whether it really achieves the required result. It will also pay to take note of the *vocal interest* in your delivery (plus your *body language*, if you're doing a video recording).

When you first begin to give presentations you might also want to set the microphone a little way away from you so that you can learn to project your voice. There are two main points of difference between *projecting* your voice and *raising* your voice (the latter is technically referred to as shouting):

1a   To project your voice you must use your *diaphragm* to drive the air up through your throat and mouth.
1b   When you shout you use your *neck muscles* to do all the work.

2a   When you project your voice, you should find that you can talk as easily as if you were conversing with someone only a short distance away. Projecting your voice should not cause any kind of physical strain.
2b   When you shout, it *hurts*!

If you have trouble learning to project your voice correctly, you may find that it is worth paying a couple of visits to a professional voice coach or singing teacher.

Finally, when you feel that you've got things almost right – stop rehearsing. To give a really good performance you must have as much interest in your presentation as you want to see in your audience, and that's not very likely if you've already rehearsed it to death.

Night and day, you are the one

The best state to be in just before you give a presentation is relaxed but alert. This may depend on whether you are a 'day person' or a 'night person'.

Day people find it easy to make an early start, but they tend to run out of steam later in the day. Night people, by contrast, may find it quite hard going to handle early morning sessions, and will be far more lively in the afternoon. If you are a night person and you have to give a presentation in the early morning, set the alarm at least a half-hour earlier than usual. This will give your body enough time to get into gear before you step into the spotlight.

For relaxation, on the other hand, you might like to consider listening to a tape of violin music by Mozart or one of the baroque composers (Vivaldi, Handel, etc), which is restful without causing drowsiness.

Don't take it personally

Be aware that there never has been, and never will be, a *perfect* presentation. Whether any particular presentation goes well or not so well, there'll always be room for improvement.

Part of the learning process can be achieved through the use of evaluation sheets to get feedback from your audience. But beware – the responses that come back can range from absurd, through helpful, to the downright destructive. It shouldn't take you too long to realise that audience evaluations should be treated as either a learning opportunity or bin fodder, with not much in between. There are few (if any) experienced presenters who don't know *exactly* what is meant by the expression: 'You can never please *all* of the people *all* of the time.'

Incidentally, these evaluation sheets should be designed to elicit *comments* rather than *ratings*. Even then, the results can be very varied, as review form comments show:

1a 'Pace too fast at times, and too in-depth in certain areas.'
1b 'Good structure, presentation and content.'

2a 'Pace generally too slow and notes do not add more detail to the lectures.'
2b 'Very detailed – lots to absorb in a day, but good notes to take away.'

3a   'Good clear concise material.'

3b   'Could do with better presentation material.'

4a   '[the presenter] covered a tremendous volume of material quickly and lucidly.'

4b   'Disappointing – felt instructor's knowledge was too limited.'

Believe it or not, as they say, these comments (which are quoted in full) all refer to four different runnings of the same one-day presentation. On all four occasions the same person was giving the presentation, using the same materials. And yet, though each *pair* of comments were written on the same day, it is clear that audience perception varied quite radically as to the quality of both the presenter *and* the presentation.

In short, even when you exercise all of the communication skills you have at your command, the people in the audience will always hear, see and evaluate the event in the light of their own personal perceptions. They might have a hangover, or maybe they rowed with their husband/wife/partner/boss/underling prior to the presentation. Or on the other hand they may have heard that they're getting a pay rise or they may just enjoy your particular style of presentation.

The trick, as explained in Chapter 4, is to know where to focus your attention. If you pay undue notice to the negative issues then presenting can become an onerous chore with very little reward. If you look *forward*, however, treating each new presentation as another opportunity to develop and hone your skills, then presenting can be one of the most rewarding aspects of business life.

Limbering up

Muscular tension can also affect your ability to speak easily and clearly. It is a good policy, therefore, to 'limber up' before you speak to get your body into the right state.

A little deep breathing is a good way to start. Make sure you get plenty of oxygen into your blood, but don't overdo it. Just three or four deep breaths will normally be sufficient to give you a bit of a lift. If you feel the least bit dizzy then stop immediately – you're probably hyperventilating and that won't help at all.

A safe way to loosen up your neck and shoulder muscles is the *Chicken Peck*.

Standing in a comfortable position, with your spine as straight as possible, slowly push your chin out so that your whole head moves forward – keeping your chin up. Then bring your head back as far as it will go, still keeping your chin at the original angle. Do this 10 or 12 times in a steady rhythm, being careful not to strain the neck muscles.

If you do feel any tightness or discomfort in the muscles at the back of your neck, sit down and tilt your head back as far as it will comfortably go and count to 20. Then straighten your head and see how your neck feels. Repeat this as often as you need to – three or four repetitions will usually be sufficient to relieve all but the very worst neck ache.

Desert mouth syndrome

Apart from forgetting what to say, nothing is worse than literally 'drying up' during a presentation. The first part of the remedy is to avoid anything that could cause 'desert mouth' syndrome. This includes salted snacks (crisps, peanuts, etc), smoking, and stimulants such as alcoholic drinks, coffee, tea and carbonated soft drinks, all of which can irritate the throat and cause 'desert mouth' syndrome.

One of the most effective ways of stimulating the production of saliva is to suck on a slice of lemon or to drink a little lemon juice. A far more practical solution is to have a supply of chilled (but definitely *not* iced) mineral water mixed with a touch of lemon or lime juice (experiment to find a balance that suits your palate). This makes a truly refreshing drink and an infallible antidote to 'desert mouth'.

A 'mighty, rushing wind'

And finally, you should also remember to avoid anything that is likely to cause flatulence or hiccups! Here, again, carbonated drinks are among the major villains, not to mention spicy foods. Do bear in mind, as well, that overeating *and* under-eating can both cause embarrassing tummy rumbles during a presentation.

Presentation checklist

So, to summarise everything we've covered, in the form of a checklist (some of the items will only apply if you are, to some extent, responsible for managing the event):

- **Are you clear about the purpose of the presentation?**
- **Have you (as far as possible) identified your audience?**
- **Is a presentation the best way (available to you) of achieving that purpose?**
- **Are you clear about what must be in the presentation to achieve the purpose?**
- **Have you decided upon a clear and appropriate structure?**
- **Have you undertaken, or have you delegated, the task of carrying out any research needed to verify any facts you intend to use?**
- **Have you prepared a script or some form of notes covering what you need to say?**
- **Have you timed the delivery of your presentation (including, if you allow audience interaction, a contingency margin of 15-20 per cent)?**

- Have you rehearsed your delivery (including memorising the first 2 minutes)?
- Have you marked your script/notes to indicate the tea/ coffee breaks?
- Have you designed and produced your visual aids?
- Have you checked any equipment you will be using (including a complete run through of all of your graphics, if any)?
- Have you checked the venue, including electrical sockets, lighting controls, location of windows, etc?
- Have you checked the location of fire exits, washrooms, etc and selected a way to convey the information to delegates?
- Have you identified the person to contact at the venue if anything goes wrong?
- Have you checked that the room will be laid out as you want it?
- Have you checked where teas and coffees will be served, and informed the person responsible for the catering as to the times of your planned breaks?

Creating Success series

Dealing with Difficult People by Roy Lilley
Decision Making & Problem Solving Strategies by John Adair
Develop Your Assertiveness by Sue Bishop
Develop Your Leadership Skills by John Adair
Develop Your NLP Skills by Andrew Bradbury
Develop Your PR Skills by Lucy Laville and Neil Richardson
Effective Customer Care by Pat Wellington
Effective Financial Management by Brian Finch
How to Deal with Stress by Stephen Palmer and Cary Cooper
How to Manage Meetings by Alan Barker
How to Manage People by Michael Armstrong
How to Motivate People by Patrick Forsyth
How to Negotiate Effectively by David Oliver
How to Sell Yourself by Ray Grose
How to Understand Business Finance by Bob Cinnamon and
    Brian Helweg-Larsen
How to Write a Business Plan by Brian Finch
How to Write a Marketing Plan by John Westwood
How to Write Reports and Proposals by Patrick Forsyth
Improve Your Coaching and Training Skills by Patrick Forsyth
Improve Your Communication Skills by Alan Barker
Organise Yourself by John Caunt
Successful Interviewing and Recruitment by Rob Yeung
Successful Presentation Skills by Andrew Bradbury
Successful Project Management by Trevor Young
Successful Time Management by Patrick Forsyth
Taking Minutes of Meetings by Joanna Gutmann
Understanding Brands by Peter Cheverton

The above titles are available from all good bookshops.
For further information on these and other Kogan Page titles, or
to order online, visit the Kogan Page website at
www.koganpage.com